THE KNIFE WAS MY LIFE

S.P. WELLS

MINERVA PRESS
MONTREUX LONDON WASHINGTON

THE KNIFE WAS MY LIFE
Copyright © S.P. Wells 1995
All rights reserved

ISBN 1 85863 282 X

First published 1995 by

MINERVA PRESS
10 Cromwell Place
London SW7 2JN

Printed in Great Britain by
Antony Rowe Ltd., Chippenham, Wiltshire

Foreword

It has been said that an autobiography should be written by a man with sufficient courage to put down truthfully and without reserve all that he really thought and felt and had done. It has also been stated that no man will ever write the true story of himself - if he did, shocked eyes would be raised to heaven.

For my part, I have attempted to be as truthful as possible, allowing for the passage of the years. Indeed, it may be thought it might have been advisable to have omitted some of the more personal details, and I may be accused of erring too much in the way of frankness; but I wanted to put down in plain simple words my impressions and emotions exactly as they struck me at the time. My purpose has been to describe my feelings and reactions arising from an unhappy childhood, blighted with a severe and demoralising speech impediment, and then an all too dismal Public School career, to be followed by nearly six years at a famous London medical school where I was exceptionally naive, and, after qualifying, the long and arduous climb up the surgeon's ladder. If it appears as though a few of the episodes mentioned cast a rather doubtful light on a member of a hospital staff, they are but rare exceptions. As Mark Twain remarked: "I am going to speak of everybody I have met exactly as I found them, nothing extenuating." Beyond a shadow of doubt the vast majority of all grades of staff gave devoted care and attention to the needs of the patients whose welfare was at all times uppermost in their minds.

To all the countless numbers of sisters and nurses who have looked after my patients so splendidly in the past, I take this opportunity to say a very sincere thank you.

Introduction

It is necessary to appreciate I was no ordinary student in this story of my experiences from the time I started as a medical student to the day I became a Consultant Surgeon many years later. I had gone through an unhappy and traumatic childhood, only to be followed by an equally unhappy and dismal school record. The youngest of three children of a country GP, for some inexplicable reason I suffered from a gross speech defect to such an extent I was mostly quite unable to make myself understood. In those distant days, if a child did not talk normally by the age of 4 or 5, he or she was considered to be suffering either from tongue-tie, (a condition almost never causing speaking difficulties, and anyway rare) or a degree of mental retardation. On the odd occasion when my Father called upon a senior colleague from the nearby town for a second opinion on one of his patients, I would be brought down from the nursery to have my tongue and throat examined. How I hated the silver spoon being placed into my mouth and pressed down on my tongue causing me to gag! The examination was always pronounced: 'nothing amiss there' and I expect the visiting doctor must have thought I was an unpleasant little boy with a dismal future. As time went by and there was no sign of improvement, it became increasingly clear to the village that the doctor's youngest child was not quite 'all there'. With hindsight it is difficult to appreciate how my parents accepted the fact that I was a backward child, and took no steps to try to rectify what was undoubtedly a gross speech defect, which if not corrected would inevitably affect my whole life. It is conceivable they feared I might be suffering from a degree of mental retardation and were loath to face up to the fact, preferring to bury their heads in the sand, or again perhaps felt disappointed and even a little ashamed of their younger son. I was left alone, presumably in the hope that as I grew older things would right themselves.

I continued to live in my own little world, hardly, if ever meeting other children. As I approached my 8th birthday I could neither read nor write, with little or no improvement in my speech. I was being given no lessons of any kind and was generally unhappy, only too conscious of my disability which resulted in a deep sense of insecurity. Curiously enough at this period I have no recollections of my relationship with my brother and sister. Being considerably older than myself I suppose they kept themselves to themselves; it is conceivable that they could, to a greater extent, understand what I was trying to say, despite my difficulties.

At this time, when I was seemingly drifting along to nowhere, with no foreseeable future and nothing being done by my parents, I had the great good fortune in attracting the attention of the Lady of the Manor, a Mrs. Milton Grange, who had come to hear about the doctor's 'backward' son. One day, which turned out to be the most important day of my life, we happened to meet quite by chance. I do not recall what transpired, but she came to a quick decision that I was not retarded in the true sense of the word. She told me years later that I had an intelligent look in my eyes, and thought perhaps something could and indeed should be done to try to correct my miserable speaking difficulties. Accordingly my mother was approached by this Good Samaritan to ask if she could have me for a couple of hours each morning to see if she could help me to speak normally. And so began a close association which was to last for two years. This splendid person was years ahead of the first speech therapist, and had it not been for her kindly intervention I doubtless would never have developed normally, and certainly could not have become a surgeon. At the time, Mrs. Milton Grange was consumed with a great sadness, as a year previously her only son had been killed in action at the Battle of the Somme. Like so many of his brother officers he had been slaughtered in the prime of his youth. In an attempt to overcome this tragic loss to some extent, Mrs. Grange was concerning herself more and more with good works in the village and surrounding neighbourhood, and it may well have been the challenge of attempting to do something worthwhile for the doctor's son which afforded an additional and unusual interest.

Initially she must have had some doubts in her mind as to whether it would be possible to get me to speak normally, especially at the age of eight, but with determination and perseverance, progress was made, although in the early stages it was slow, at times painfully so.

Although it is now so long ago I remember quite clearly that first morning going to the big Manor house. I recall the walk up the tree-lined drive a full quarter of a mile long, the sight of the imposing house when it came into view, and my hesitation in ringing the front door bell. Hopelessly shy and withdrawn, I entered the large and imposing hall with fearful anxiety, finding myself in an environment totally alien. At first I must have been in awe of my new found friend. Fortunately for me she possessed a tremendously strong personality and having made up her mind to take on a task, however difficult, there could be no question of turning back. In no time at all Mrs. Milton Grange discovered I was extremely short-sighted - indeed I could see nothing clearly unless it was held close to my face, due to congenital myopia unrecognised by anyone until now. As I had never been able to see anything unless close to hand, I had no real appreciation that my vision was so defective. Having no standards of comparison, or example of what you have never had you never miss. I remember being taken to Eastbourne during the war years, and standing on the promenade amongst a crowd who, I was told, were intent on watching a submarine anchored close in shore. I was unable to see anything at all, but in my child's mind reasoned that it was because of my age. I was still too young to see what the grown-ups were looking at. When I grew older I would also be able to see the submarine and be able to participate in the other privileges enjoyed by my elders. Considering I had been born very severely myopic, this line of reasoning seemed to have been sensible enough, but it is difficult to explain how my parents so dismally failed to spot my defective eyesight. Possibly it was contributed to my general backwardness - just another manifestation of a slow or retarded process of development. My grossly defective vision having at last been spotted, I was sent to an eye specialist who prescribed the necessary glasses - in those days in round ugly metal frames. The eye specialist found it hard to understand how it came about that a doctor's son had been so badly neglected with regard to his sight. Wearing my new glasses I entered almost another world - for the first time in my life I could see things I had never visualised before, and the sight of distant objects was a thrilling experience opening up whole new horizons.

Slowly but surely, and entirely due to my guardian angel's sheer determination and outstanding personality and intelligence, I at last began to talk so as to be understood. This however was not accomplished without a great deal of effort on both our parts, and at times considerable distress on mine. There were days when I seemed to be making no progress. However despite the almost inevitable disappointments and set backs, as the weeks and months passed, steady progress was made, and after a year I was able to speak in a normal way.

I was now nine years of age, could neither read nor write and even the simplest lessons were quite beyond my capabilities. Having succeeded so brilliantly in her speech therapy, as it would now be termed, Mrs. Milton Grange felt she would like to continue her good work and accordingly embarked on daily lessons literally starting from scratch, for despite my late age, up to this time no attempt had been made to teach me anything. Nothing daunted her! She set about the task with her usual determination, and to such good effect that after a year's intensive work it was considered I had reached the point when thought should be given to the idea of my going to school as I had now reached the age of ten. It was decided I should be sent to a public school nearby, starting off in the preparatory school, known as 'The Inky'. I was anything but keen on the idea. Although by this time I had completely overcome my speaking difficulties, I remained totally lacking in self confidence, was painfully shy, had never mixed with boys of my own age, and had no friends. My parents who were anything but happily married were of little help. It was with fear in my heart that I approached the 'Inky' that first morning. I felt so very much alone. I felt totally inadequate and dreaded having to mix with all the other boys. As I passed through the gate, alone, and feeling very self-conscious in my new school uniform, the red brick buildings appeared large and forbidding to my fearful eyes, and I was filled with acute apprehension as to what ordeals lay ahead. I had never before been in such awe-inspiring surroundings and I felt utterly at sea.

In the early 1920's Public Schools were hell-bent on games which were at all times compulsory, and popularity with the other boys was almost exclusively based on prowess on the playing fields. To be Captain of the First XV was to be hero worshipped. Not having played any games I was yet again at a great disadvantage. At this time very few boys wore spectacles and I was quickly dubbed 'four eyes', and was in constant fear of having my glasses knocked off and broken.

As was to be expected my school days were unhappy times. Apart from being a complete duffer as far as sport was concerned I was in addition nearly always close to the bottom of the form and came to dread passing through the gates each morning, wondering what fresh ordeals lay ahead. I made no real friends and continued to be withdrawn and totally lacking in confidence. It is no wonder I was a gross misfit in a large public school where boys' popularity rested so exclusively on their achievements on the playing fields. I just could not hope to compete.

It was an enormous relief when the time came to leave school to embark on my medical training. I had not been asked if I wanted to become a doctor, it was just decided I should follow in my Father's footsteps with a view to taking over the practice in due course, always provided I could manage to pass the necessary examinations, which at this stage looked in doubt. It was against this inconspicuous background that I embarked on my medical career. I was soon to discover I had a great deal to learn about the 'facts of life'.

Chapter One

The day I began my medical career is as clear in my mind today as though it were only yesterday despite it being well over fifty five years ago. At 17 years of age I was introverted, extremely unsure of myself and immeasurably immature. Breakfasting at an early hour I arrived too soon at the station, and sitting in the train on the way to London wondered how I would make out at a large and famous medical college, having made such a mess of my days at a public school. Furthermore I was not really sure I wanted to become a doctor and viewed the days ahead with some dismay. I had not been adequately consulted on this all important matter, it was merely assumed I would be following in my Father's footsteps and in the course of time would be in a position to take over his practice. To do this I must get my medical degree; the why's and wherefore's were not discussed.

At the time it was not difficult to gain entrance to a medical school, which was fortunate as far as I was concerned, for there was nothing approaching the tremendous competition of the present day intelligence tests and the requirement of many 'A' levels were far into the future. Had this been so at the time I applied I would not have stood even the remotest chance of a place, in view of my extremely poor past record. As it was, following my application, I received a letter requesting me to attend for an interview with the Dean of the Medical School - an interview of which I only have but a vague recollection. I do recall being treated with courtesy, and being put at my ease by the Dean, an eminent Harley Street Physician. A few days later, I received a letter informing me that I had been accepted as a medical student for the coming year. I imagine the Dean must have been a very understanding man, and my being the son of a doctor presumably helped. Back in those days there were very few grants. Practically all the students were dependent on their parents meeting the fees and other expenses incurred, and this was a deciding factor in limiting the number of applications.

I knew next to nothing of London, and apart from the one occasion when I had attended for my interview with the Dean of the College, I had never been there alone and certainly not in a rush hour. Nor had I been accustomed to having much in the way of loose change in my pocket. Waiting in the crowd to purchase a 2d. (old pennies) ticket for the underground was a frustrating new experience, and when at last it came to my turn, in my haste and agitation, instead of putting two pennies into the machine, by a stupid mistake I mistook a half crown for a penny piece. So in place of a second penny in went 2/6. Not until I had jammed the machine did I realise my mistake and then it was too late! The queue behind me was considerable and becoming restive at the unseen delay, so feeling an utter fool at wasting so much money, (in those days half a crown was a lot of money) and having no wish to let the ever lengthening queue know it was all my fault that they were unable to get their tickets and the wait had been in vain, I retreated to another machine. When my turn eventually came I made doubly sure it was two pennies I inserted. My first underground ticket had proved to be both expensive and traumatic and it was anything but an auspicious start.

On reaching the medical school I entered through an ancient and impressive gateway to be met by a well turned out elderly man who clearly commanded authority and respect. Thinking, on my first day, I must show suitable respect for my superiors, I addressed this seemingly august person with due decorum, adding 'sir' at what I considered suitable intervals. I had barely recovered from the shock of the ticket episode, and now what little self confidence I possessed was dealt a further blow on discovering that I had been addressing the head porter in the mistaken belief I had been talking to at least the sub-Dean.

I was relieved to find that my fellow first year students (or freshers) appeared a pleasant lot, at least at first sight. In those days women were not admitted, there being a strong feeling against female medics in the hospital. Periodically the question would be raised as to whether this was really fair and reasonable, and perhaps they should be allowed though in limited numbers. This idea was always flatly rejected, and to clinch the decision it was ruled as being quite impracticable as there would be no lavatory accommodation available - this being considered an insurmountable objection. As it was, our cloak room was no great shakes - a dark and somewhat dismal place reached by a flight of ageing stone steps. The accommodation as a whole was very far from luxurious, the common room being sparsely furnished, and the refectory (known as the Rec) sited in the basement, having but the bare essentials. The food however was adequate and by present day prices amazingly cheap. Two sausages and mash cost only six old pennies, and a satisfying lunch could be had for 11½d. and this with waitress service. Two bananas and real cream cost 6d. and was looked upon as almost an extravagance. The Honorary Physicians and Surgeons, or Chiefs as they were called, also used the Rec, separate tables being set apart for the Mighty. (At that time the Specialist medical staff received no remuneration for their hospital work, their income coming from private practice, hence the term Honorary.) I looked upon these great men eating their sausage and mash with considerable awe, wondering what it must feel like to be in their exalted position, and wondering still more if I would even qualify let alone become a specialist surgeon or physician. At this stage there loomed so many obstacles in the way ahead.

Taken as a whole the students' behaviour was good. Indeed it had to be at that time for discipline was still considered necessary although no longer at school. Disruptions such as sit-ins and wilful damage to property were unheard of, and if anything of this nature had taken place it would have been immediately dealt with. Provided a student behaved in a reasonable manner, and provided his fees were met, he could remain for an almost indefinite period - indeed in my time there was one perpetual medical student who had been many years at the hospital and still had not qualified. He more or less looked upon the place as a kind of London club, and having private means, was in no hurry to leave the hospital. He spent more time playing bridge than attending to his medical studies. He was a nice enough fellow, though he had a tiresome habit of setting newspapers alight. His technique was simple, on seeing someone engrossed in reading the Times or Daily Telegraph he would quietly approach, and with a cigarette lighter set a corner of the paper alight. At first unaware of what was happening, the unsuspecting reader would suddenly be confronted with a sheet of flame. This called for prompt action, and necessitated quickly discarding the burning newsprint and stamping out the flames on the parquet floor. I personally looked upon this as a foolish if not indeed dangerous practice, apart from spoiling a copy of the daily newspapers. Although I saw this happen on numerous occasions I never witnessed any harm. It was supposed to test the victim's reflexes - he certainly had to jump to it!

As with all first year medics I was anxious to witness my first major operation and to see if I could take it. In the pre-clinical years we were not allowed into the actual theatre itself, but could go into the observation gallery at any time provided we had nothing better to do. These galleries were constructed so as to allow a good view through a glass screen of the theatre beneath, though the actual operating table was some distance away. This did not hinder, however, observing the team at work or appreciating the general atmosphere, all eyes naturally being focused on the surgeon. I wondered what my initial reaction would be at my first sight of blood in any quantity and whether or not I would disgrace myself by having to leave the gallery, or even worse by passing out, for I had heard such varied accounts of what could happen. When I entered I saw that the patient had already been anaesthetised in a separate room, and was now being carefully placed on the operating table with one arm outstretched at right angles to the body. The positioning of the patient appeared to be important and took a little while, the specialist anaesthetist with an anaesthetic clerk, paying careful attention to the head end. The patient was breathing deeply but evenly, the head covered with a white cap. Even at this stage the atmosphere was heavy with ether and antiseptics, and I thought I could discern a certain tension in the theatre. When all appeared to be to his satisfaction, the surgeon turned towards the watching students and gave a brief summary of the case, outlining the steps of the operation he was about to perform. Not all the surgeons were as helpful; some tended to ignore the spectators which was reasonable enough, as at this early stage few, if any, had a real grasp of what was taking place, being largely first year students. Two years or more would elapse before starting clinical work in the wards and theatre proper.

To return to the operation - the surgeon explained that he was operating on the patient because she had a large and indefinite mass in the left breast which was certainly a cancer, and he was going to remove the whole breast together with the underlying structures, hoping thereby to eradicate the disease. There she lay, the upper half of her body exposed, one arm outstretched, the other by her side. From the distance of the gallery, the tumour could not be visualised, and it seemed such a shame that one of her breasts had to be sacrificed. There they were, round and shapely, moving up and down with each anaesthetised breath, under the glare of the operating light. An assistant painted the skin overlying the breasts and chest wall with a solution of iodine. What was previously virgin flesh now became stained with an ugly brown coloration, ragged at the edges where the iodine had dripped from the swab. Sterile towels were next placed to cover the patient's body, the operation area only being left exposed. So far I had watched with interest and had not felt the least bit upset, but the true test was yet to come. Having asked the anaesthetist if it was alright to start, the surgeon was handed a scalpel by the theatre sister, and pressing much harder than I had imagined, made a long and sweeping cut in the skin surrounding the doomed breast. I had thought that immediately the knife was applied blood would at once begin to flow from the edges of the incision. But this was not the case. Only after a few seconds did a slow trickle start where the knife had done its work, though in no time at all the trickle turned into copious bleeding from the spurting blood vessels. This deluge of blood had been anticipated by placing a towel on the floor beside the operating table - initially so clean and white, it rapidly changed to a gory red as the ever flowing blood continued to be absorbed. As the operation progressed so did the bleeding, and there was even blood on the surgeon's forehead which had got in the way of a spurting vessel. I felt no sense of nausea, only revulsion that such mutilation was deemed necessary. The surgeon continued to work surely and swiftly, clipping the larger bleeding vessels with forceps, and then tying them with cat gut ligatures. As the dissection continued, the underlying ribs came into view and the extensive wound appeared to be a sea of blood. Finally the breast was severed from the patient and the bleeding arrested. This last took longer than I had anticipated as there seemed so many vessels to stop. Having satisfied himself that there were no more bleeders he stitched up the long and extensive incision and at the conclusion of the operation the sister applied a massive dressing having first swabbed the congealed blood away from the surrounding skin. Again the patient was lifted carefully onto a trolley and wheeled out of the theatre, still deeply unconscious and looking very pale and fragile. As she left the nurses started to mop up the blood from the floor, the surgeon peeled off his gloves and gown and prepared for his next case.

It is now over fifty five years since I watched the operation which I have just described in some detail, and it must have made a strong impression on me for my memory is so clear. I really had only a vague idea what a major surgical operation would entail and I had not anticipated such a traumatic procedure. As it happened I had seen one of the bloodiest cases. There were many other operations far less awe-inspiring. I suppose it is only to be expected that I should not have forgotten such a major event in the earliest days of my student career, for the reaction to the sight of blood in any quantity, until put to the test, is an unknown factor. It is for this reason I have written of the various stages of a major operation as it struck me, seeing it all for the first time and little knowing what to expect. I remember feeling a sense of great relief that I had not been physically disturbed, the more so because I could hardly have picked on a more traumatic one. The sight of all that blood left me quite unmoved. However, two of my fellow students were nauseated by what they witnessed, and another was forced to make a hasty exit from the gallery. To me, who had failed so often and at so many things, to have survived this my first test with ease, and even better than some, was a most welcome boost to my ego, and for once I felt pleased with myself. I hasten to add that such mutilating operations have not been performed for many years - they belong to the remote past.

When I reached home that evening I related in some detail the steps of the operation I had just witnessed to my Father. I suppose I must, for this once, still have been feeling pleased with myself. He told me he had seen an exactly similar case on his first visit to an operating theatre in Edinburgh towards the end of the last century - an era when surgery was not nearly in such an advanced state as in the 1920's. In place of a towel to mop up the blood spilling on the floor, he had seen sawdust used, and the surgeons of the time wore neither sterile gowns or gloves. The usual procedure on entering the theatre, which resembled a large lecture hall rather than a modern operating room, was to take off the morning coat (the habitual dress of the time) hang it on a hook on the theatre door, and to take down in its place a short operating jacket, which was seldom washed from one week to another. Indeed, the more blood stained the coat, the more experienced the surgeon was considered to be - a clean jacket might well denote a lack of experience. A well known surgeon of the time never failed to transfer his button hole, which was more often than not a rose, from his morning coat to his operating jacket, and took great care that it was not soiled by a spurting blood vessel. Indeed if there was a danger of this occurring he would at once tell his assistant 'to mind the flower', and was most upset if the flower became blooded.

If, by modern standards, the surgery of that time was crude, the anaesthetics were little or no further advanced. Instead of a small room where the patient, justifiably terrified at the thought of the impending operation, could be anaesthetised prior to being brought into the theatre itself, they were instead carried into the operating arena in a long wicker basket by four medical students, and then chloroform was administered on the operating table. Once under the anaesthetic speed was considered all important, and a surgeon's dexterity came to be judged by the time he took to perform the operation. When opening an abdomen the rule was: 'Quick in and quicker out'. The great danger at this time was sepsis. Aseptic surgery was yet to come and nearly all the wounds became heavily infected, and the mortality was high.

To get back to my student days. Although great advances had already been made since my Father's time in Edinburgh, greater and far more reaching advances still lay in the future. Having seen my first operation I did not often return to the gallery, as the days were mostly taken up with lectures in chemistry, physics and biology, leaving little time for anything not immediately concerned with passing the examination at the end of the first year, so enabling us to proceed to the study of anatomy and physiology. Taken as a whole the lectures and demonstrations were good, though one of the senior lecturers in biology was more than tedious, insisting on his lectures being written down in full, as he spoke at dictation speed, and each week our note books had to be handed in for correction. It was just like being back at school.

As well as being tedious, he was also a pompous little man, with a trim goatee beard, and full of his own importance. On one occasion, a Saturday, someone must have misbehaved. I have simply no recollection of this misdemeanour. Without further ado he stormed out of the room in anger, telling us as he did so that he was not used to lecturing to a crowd of ill-behaved animals. He only lectured to gentlemen. Furthermore there would be no resumption until an apology was forthcoming. This was a real threat, for it was essential that at the end of the session his signature be obtained stating that attendance had been entirely satisfactory. I suppose an apology must have been received for the lectures resumed next week. This was long in the past, but how very different from the present generation of students! I know at the time I was vexed for I had had the sweat of making a round journey of 100 miles for a lecture which lasted a matter of minutes.

The journey of 100 miles came about as it was decided I should continue to live at home, travelling each day to London by train. This entailed getting up at an early hour, cycling two miles to the station, a train journey of fifty miles, and then on reaching town, taking the underground to the nearest station to the hospital; a matter of ten minutes walk away. This tedious journey had of course to be repeated at the end of a day's work. For the first year this extensive travelling schedule had to be undertaken six days a week for the Saturday morning's lecture, attendance at which was compulsory.

In the early stage in the career of a medical student, it was most unwise to cut lectures. A strict register was kept and great importance placed on a good record of attendance. Later on, as we progressed to clinical lectures, a board would be passed round, each student being required to sign his name on the attendance sheet. Now it was possible to ask a friend to 'sign you up' if you wished to cut the lecture. All he had to do was to sign his own name and then yours in a different hand. The classes were large and the discrepancy went unnoticed.

Initially I found the long distance travelling tiring and interfering with my studies, but in the course of time I came to accept the long train journeys, and was able to study in the mornings, though usually too tired to do so on the return journey, often falling asleep. In the winter months it could be cold and often wet, and a cycle ride of two miles to the station in pouring rain made a bad start for a long day. It is quite surprising how wet, even over a comparatively short distance, one can get on a bicycle. At these times I must have arrived looking far from spic and span. Medical students in those days, although having the everlasting reputation of notorious living, were expected to look tidily dressed. Later on, when (in layman's terms) we were walking the wards, we were expected to wear suits. No question of the casual clothes and sandals of the present era.

For practically all my time as a student I lived at home, travelling up to town daily, though towards the end I had a short period living in digs in London. So long ago there was no question of any residential accommodation attached to the medical school - hostels and halls of residence were very much in the future. It is with not a little satisfaction I am able to look back and recall that I never once missed a train; I took care to be on time. The trains of that period ran to schedule, and were seldom late except during periods of fog in the winter, when delays could be considerable, and I would sit impatiently in my compartment knowing I could not possibly arrive in time for my first lecture.

For practical biology we dissected in turn the earth worm, the frog and the dog fish. The worm was killed by being placed in a jar containing alcohol and then dissected, the cut edges being pinned to a board - the earth worm has a simple structure. Next came the frog which was killed by chloroform and was a more complex creature, and lastly the dog fish, still more complex. Rubber gloves were not worn, and after spending some time dissecting the fish, our hands became impregnated with an unpleasant and persistent smell. This I was to find even more distasteful when I came to enter the anatomy rooms for dissection of the human body. Even so, I found the long persisting aroma of dead fish particularly unattractive - it appeared literally to be skin deep. I removed an eye from my specimen to take home, presumably so I could show my Father what I had dissected. I so clearly remember producing it out of my pocket at our evening meal, and rolling it across the polished dining room table to where my Father was sitting, very much to his annoyance! The eye, or more accurately, the lens of the eye, was hard and shiny and spherical, and rolled along as does a marble, coming to rest at the side of his dinner plate.

Not content with bringing home a specimen from a dissected dog fish I proceeded to demonstrate my newly acquired knowledge of the earth worm to the Lady of the Manor, Mrs. Milton Grange, who in the past had been so wonderful in helping me to overcome a major speaking difficulty which at the time threatened to mar my young life. I still continued to see Mrs. Milton Grange from time to time so I thought she would be interested to be shown a specimen of my recent work, I found a nice fat juicy worm, killed it in the usual way by immersing it in methylated spirit, and proceeded with the dissection, pinning apart the cut edges on a small wooden box. When I had finished I felt well pleased with my work which I considered to be well up to standard. Mounting my bicycle, holding the opened worm carefully in one hand, I proceeded to the Manor house. When a maid answered my ring at the front door I handed in my prize specimen with the request that she should give it to Mrs. Milton Grange. At the time it never entered my head that the maid might not like to handle such an unusual package, or that Mrs. Milton Grange might well not wish to receive such an exhibit. Looking back on this episode it now seems to have been a quite extraordinary thing to do, but at that time I was still terribly immature. I well remember when I next saw Mrs. Milton Grange she told me she would prefer not to see any more of my dissections!

That first year passed without any undue incidents, and although I found it tiresome and at times tiring, I was becoming used to travelling backwards and forwards each day to London. In the pre-clinical years we had quite long holidays at Christmas, Easter and in the summer. It was with much relief that I heard I had passed the first year examinations, especially as I felt I had not done too well in one of the practicals. I could now proceed to more interesting subjects - namely anatomy and physiology. Still not one hundred percent certain that I wanted to be a doctor, I was happy enough to be a member of a famous medical school, and I was in fact slowly gaining confidence in myself, though I still had a long way to go.

Chapter Two

Before starting in the dissecting room, the senior anatomist gave a short pep talk. The only thing I can recall was an assurance that should we accidentally cut our hands whilst dissecting, no harm would accrue and there would be no question of contracting blood poisoning as the bodies had been injected with carbolic for preservation. This was long before the discovery of antibiotics. The anatomy course was to last for well over a year - in actual fact I think it was eighteen months. The bodies for dissection were to be divided into parts - arms, legs, abdomen, thorax, head, neck and brain, and we were required to pass an oral examination on each part before we could proceed to the next. I had not previously come face to face with death and wondered what my first reactions would be on entering the anatomy room. This proved to be, as I had anticipated, a grim place with bare walls, stone floor, and a glass panelled roof for maximum light, and row upon row of stiff naked bodies lying on white slabs awaiting the students' clumsy attempts at dissection. The whole atmosphere stank of carbolic mingled with death, and was little short of awe-inspiring. I am sure if I were to enter such a room now I would experience a deep sense of pity for those bodies lying so forlorn and forgotten, and would wonder what sort of life they had lived and what brought them to their present resting place. In those days the supply of bodies was adequate - for one thing there was nothing like the number of medical students as at present, and for another many died in poor law institutions. If their bodies were not claimed by relatives they found their way to the medical schools. In addition a few left in their wills a request that their bodies should be used to further medical education. As far as I can recall after such a length of time, I experienced no feelings of revulsion at being so intimately concerned with death, rather a sense of awe and bewilderment at the prospect of what lay before me - it was all so very strange.

We worked in pairs - two to an arm, two to a leg and so on. We had to provide our own white coats, and there was never any question of wearing rubber gloves for the protection of our hands. The coats were not washed for the whole of the term and quickly became smelly, dirty and greasy with the fat from the corpses; though these had of course been adequately preserved. It was some time before I became used to leaving the dissecting room and going to the refectory, for the smell of carbolic mingled with death remained on my hands despite repeated washing and scrubbing, and I seemed to taste carbolic in my food. I can still vividly recall the first time I ate a piece of bread and butter at tea. Having come straight from the anatomy room, at first I could not make out what was amiss then it dawned on me that the cause lay in my hands. This was readily confirmed, for on smelling them there was a strong odour of carbolic. As time went by I came to notice this less and less. But I was ever conscious of the all pervading smell of disinfectant which lingered on after every visit to the dissecting room, even though I washed and washed again.

My initial attempts at dissection, I remember, started with a leg, and were ineffectual in the extreme. I had never before held a surgical knife, and did not appreciate how hard you had to press to cut through the skin, especially in a preserved body, nor did I know where exactly to start, nor indeed what to do having made a cut. The many nerves, arteries and even muscles are not easy to define by the inexperienced, and it was only too easy to cut through a structure before it had been recognised. We took it in turns to dissect - the one not so employed reading out the instructions from the anatomy manual; if an important nerve or artery was inadvertently destroyed, and one which it was necessary to preserve, recriminations would sometimes follow, but always in a friendly spirit. Demonstrators would come round at intervals to check on our dissections and were distressed if the various structures had not been adequately exposed, and even more so if they had been mistakenly cut away.

To start with, the leg allocated was still attached to the body, so initially there were a number of students working on the one body - two to each leg and arm and two to the abdomen and thorax. At this stage it was not possible for all of us to work at the same time. As the dissecting progressed the limbs were removed and taken to other side tables where the dissecting continued in much less crowded conditions. The anatomy books, so valuable for giving directions as to how to proceed, quickly became soiled with grease from the dead parts, indeed nearly everything got contaminated.

In addition to dissecting a body we also had to acquire a skeleton for the study of the bones in detail. Once again we discovered some of the long bones were surprisingly greasy. Although we were left to a large extent to our own initiative, anatomy demonstrators were always available, and on request would come and advise and even help with our dissections. When we felt we had acquired the necessary knowledge they would arrange for a viva to see if we were considered fit to proceed to the next stage.

In addition to the demonstrators, who were hoping to become surgeons in due course and who were in the process of acquiring the all important and essential Fellowship of the Royal College of Surgeons, there was a Professor of Anatomy in overall charge who was held in high esteem, and who kept a constant watch on his department, ensuring that it maintained a satisfactorily high standard.

As I have mentioned, were I to return to the anatomy rooms now, with hindsight I would give more thought to the quality of life the dismembered bodies had experienced, how much happiness as opposed to sadness had been their lot, and what trials and suffering they had endured, and finally, if life had dealt them a fair deal. I would also ponder further over the circumstances which had caused the corpses to end up on a bare stone table in a medical school, and the possibility, or more likely the probability, that they had had a lonely death with no loved ones for support at the end. For them at last the imponderable question of the Afterlife, so impossible to solve in the living, would now be resolved in death.

If I were to dissect again an arm or a leg, as the various muscles came into view, only in turn to be sacrificed in order to display the further structures beneath, I would think back to the days when they were living tissues capable of the most intricate movements as well as participating in many an amorous embrace. And now, there they lay, still and stiff and useless, being systematically destroyed by an inexperienced student wielding a blunted knife. But I was young, in those days, and cannot recall giving much thought, if indeed any, to what had at one time been a living human being. I saw it more as a challenge to complete the course and to pass the necessary examinations - a hurdle which had to be surmounted before a start could be made with clinical medicine. Dealing with living patients would be a most welcome change from the prolonged study of the dead. Although not completely sure that I wanted to be a doctor, I certainly wanted to go into the hospital wards and leave behind the tedious studies of the pre-clinical years. I wished very much to change the classroom for the wards.

As well as Anatomy, Physiology also had to be passed before this could happen. I cannot remember much about the course for it lacked the drama of the dissecting room. It consisted of the usual lectures and demonstrations, the time being more or less spent equally between anatomy and physiology, and at the end of the eighteen months an examination had to be taken in both subjects. When the time drew near I was not unduly worried and thought I stood a fair chance of a pass, and on the day of the examination considered I had written reasonable papers. However, when I came away from the examination hall and had an opportunity of discussing with my fellow students how they had answered certain questions, I was horrified to discover that I had misread one of the questions in physiology and had written on quite the wrong subject - a most stupid mistake and one which would clearly bring me no marks at all. I was, only naturally, exceedingly annoyed with myself, not to say extremely worried as to the result, for I feared I would now have failed in this subject. I awaited the result with apprehension, the more so because I felt I had not shown up too well when it came to the viva. In due course I was notified of the results by letter - I opened this with trembling fingers, knowing it would be a near miracle if I had passed, and miracles just did not happen, at least not when it came to examination results. It was as I had anticipated - a pass in anatomy and a failure in physiology. I feared my Father would be far from pleased when I showed him the letter, but he was not really much put out as he told me that he also had ploughed in this subject in Edinburgh. This was his only failure and was happily to be so in my case also. Our medical student days seemed to be running a parallel course - we had both seen an amputation of a breast as our first operation and now we had similar failures in physiology.

Having failed in this subject I had a further three months to put in before resitting the examination. I had made quite certain on this occasion to read the questions carefully, and not to be such a stupid ass again, and I also acquitted myself reasonably well in the viva. When it came to opening the envelope announcing the result, I did so with much more confidence and was much relieved to find that I had passed. I could at long last set forth for clinical studies in the wards, dealing for the first time with living people as opposed to dead and mutilated specimens.

Chapter Three

When I first entered the medical school I had looked with envy at the senior students, resplendent in white jackets, walking across the hospital square with stethoscopes and torches prominently displayed about their persons, so clearly indicating that they were involved in real medicine. It seemed, at that time, a far distant goal to aim for, but now at last it had come to pass, and I could barely wait to purchase the stethoscope and shiny bright pocket torch which my new status demanded. I confess, when travelling by tube or train, I was careful to arrange for my newly acquired stethoscope to protrude from a coat pocket so all could see I was a budding medic and, who knows, even a fully blown doctor - it gave me a sense of importance. I even tried writing the magic word 'Dr.' in front of my name to see how it would look in black and white, though I realised only too well that I still had far to travel before this final goal could be achieved. Even at this comparatively late stage I was still not completely happy in the choice of my career, though steadily coming to terms with the idea of devoting my life to medicine. Fortunately, this was to grow at an ever increasing rate, and when I finally qualified I was quite certain I had landed, though not from my own choice, in the right profession, and as the years passed I appreciated more and more that I would not have wanted to do anything else other than become a doctor. But this is looking to the future. At the time I must still have been extremely immature for my years and certainly quite naive. I remember so well being afraid of having a wet dream the night prior to sitting an examination, for I had the stupid idea that this could adversely affect my performance, and how relieved I was on waking in the morning to find my pyjama trousers had a clean bill of health. I remained incredibly ignorant on all matters appertaining to sex and equally ill-informed in the use of certain words. On one occasion I used the word 'sod' in front of a nurse, not in the least understanding what it meant, and it was only after a kindly fellow student tactfully implied that it was not really quite the thing that I looked up the meaning in the Oxford dictionary and was mortified by my gaffe.

Having reached the stage of walking the wards, as clinical work was and perhaps still is so termed, I had now to begin to learn how to develop an understanding of the apprehensions and real fears which the patients so frequently experience. More important I had to begin to understand how to communicate in straightforward words, appreciating how they must feel at being parted from their homes and families. In short, to learn to put myself in the place of my patients - so essential to becoming a real caring doctor. At first, as was only to be expected, I felt awkward and ill at ease and realised only too plainly that the patients looked upon the young medical gentlemen as little short of student laddies and not to be taken seriously. I was much encouraged however on being told that it took a considerable time, coupled with experience, before an easy and natural approach to the patients' problems was achieved. All that mattered was to work to this end, and aim to become a personal doctor as opposed to a medical technician, this very excellent advice I have ever since tried to follow.

Our time in the wards was divided into periods each of three months. My first clinical attachment was to a surgical firm under the direction of the Professor of Surgery, a strict disciplinarian if ever there was one, and an absolute stickler for punctuality. For his ward rounds, which took place twice a week, we lined up outside the ward waiting for the Great Man to arrive, to be followed by his registrar and house surgeons, and to be met at the door by the sister, staff nurse and senior nurse. Punctually at two o'clock the retinue would enter the ward and the door would be closed. If by a mischance a dresser (this was the name by which students attached to the surgical units or firms were known - on the medical forms the word clerk was used) happened to be late, possibly by only a few minutes, he would not be allowed in, his name being recorded as absent. If this happened more than twice in the three month appointment, the unfortunate dresser would be required to do the three months all over again and this would inevitably delay the time he could sit the final examinations.

We were allocated our own patients by one of the house surgeons and were expected to write very full case histories, to carry out a complete examination and to attempt to make a definite diagnosis. On the rounds we had to read out our notes which were, more often than not, criticised by the Professor. I remember on one occasion, when a somewhat happy-go-lucky dresser had written what the Chief considered to be a very bad history, and after he had finished, asked the, by now, harassed student how many marks he would expect to score had it been an examination. Before there was any time to reply, the Professor seized the notes and started to tear them up in small pieces, remarking as he did so: 'not a single mark, this is all they are good for', as he threw the fragments away. I can see the bits of paper yet scattered over the spotless polished parquet floor as we moved to the next bed.

In those far-off days the patients awaiting an operation were clothed in a special operating gown which was a loose fitting garment open at the back, a white cap to cover the head, and on the bed table a pair of thick woollen socks, together with a small tray containing a vomit bowl and mouth gag. I always thought these appurtenances to be somewhat of a frightening sight for the already frightened patient. The Professor, who had served with distinction in the Great War, appeared to have no such thoughts for on seeing a patient thus prepared and waiting to go to the operating theatre, he would invariably go to the bedside and in a breezy manner remark, "I see you are going over the top this afternoon." Even in my experience I considered this was not a very tactful remark as so very many, in the '14 - '18 war, on going over the top had never lived to return to the trenches. And I was sure the patients would not be reassured and did silently wonder if they would see their bed again.

As well as working in the wards, we spent a lot of time watching operations - no longer sitting in the relatively remote gallery, but standing in the body of the theatre itself. At first I found it difficult not to touch all the numerous trolleys and bowls which were covered with sterile towels. It was all too easy to brush against one or the other, especially as there were always a number of dressers present, in addition to the theatre staff proper. If this happened the whole area became contaminated, and it was of the utmost importance that this error be detected and changed at once, or sepsis in the operation wound would certainly follow. On first entering the theatre, unused to wearing a cap, a mask covering the nose and mouth, gown and rubber boots, every thing felt unreal as if in a strange land. It was only too easy to brush against a sterile area especially when trying to get out of the way of one of the surgical team. I was duly sent out of the theatre on my first or second visit for touching a sterile trolley. In an attempt not to be in the way of the anaesthetised patient, who was being wheeled on a trolley from the anaesthetic room to the operating table, I stepped back and in so doing caught the edge of a table on which all the sterile instruments had been neatly laid out in orderly rows, all ready to be handed to the surgeon who was waiting to start the operation. After all these years I cannot attempt to remember what the irate theatre sister said to me at the time but it must have been very far from complimentary and she surely must have thought of me as being the lowest form of student life, for as a result of my carelessness the instruments all had to be re-sterilised and the start of the operation considerably delayed. I was banned from the theatre for the afternoon. It taught me a lesson which I was never to forget and I was more than careful not to make such a disastrous mistake again. The theatre sister wielded great power over the students, and they had to do as she said when in her domain, and this authority also extended to the nurses. The discipline was strict, as it had to be in such a high risk intensive field. There were no wonder drugs of the present day to combat wound infections, which could on occasions prove fatal.

As dressers we did not 'scrub up' as it was called, unless it was one of our own cases being operated upon. We just stood around and watched, though it was usually difficult to see clearly what was actually going on. There were so many people around the operating table, and there was the ever present danger of contaminating the sterile surrounds, all too easy to do in an attempt to obtain a closer view. If, on the other hand, the operation was to be on one of our patients, we were expected to scrub up and to act as third assistant or even fourth assistant. This entailed nothing more than standing a little distance away from the patient, behind the surgeon and chief assistant, and holding an instrument of little or no importance at odd intervals. When I was first called to assist I found it far from easy to get my sterile rubber gloves on. We had first to scrub our hands and arms under running water for a full five minutes, then put on a long white, sterile gown, and lastly the gloves and this is what I found tricky. The fingers had a habit of sticking together, and if not gently handled, of splitting, rendering the gloves useless. Naturally, as students, we were allocated the older pairs which were nearing the end of their useful life and so all the more liable to tear. There was a special technique of slipping on the gloves which we had to acquire. Having just powdered the hands, the aim was to avoid touching the outside of the gloves with the bare hand, none too easy until one had mastered the correct movements. When the gloves were on they had to be skin tight in fit. It was by no means unusual for the odd finger end to project rather after the fashion of a condom. Once the gloves were on in the approved manner, it was essential not to get the hands contaminated by touching anything unsterile. To begin with it was difficult to remember the simple basic fact that any irritation on the face would, by reflex action, cause a hand to seek the source, as it happened to me the first day I had scrubbed up. My mask felt as if it was tickling the end of my nose, and without further ado up went my hand to scratch. I had not as yet learned to control my reflexes. The ever vigilant theatre-sister at once spotted this gross mistake, and after she had said her piece, I never did it again. I was learning how very important it is to discipline yourself at the outset, and I have been ever thankful that I was brought up in a tough school with high standards - we certainly had to toe the line and no nonsense.

As I have said we scrubbed up only when our case was on the table. We did not change into operating clothes, merely removed our collars and ties, kept on shirts and trousers over which we wore the sterile gowns. We really played no part in the operation and were nearly always standing a little away from the patient - in this position we were an easy target for what was known as the 'trousers game'. A student, not scrubbed up would quietly approach from behind and undo one of the buttons of the braces, whilst from the other side a second student would undo the remaining one. The operation gowns were open at the back and it was an easy matter to reach the buttons. With both undone the trousers would begin to slip down, though this could be counteracted to some extent by separating the legs ever wider. The surgeon and his assistants were too busy with the operation to notice anything outside their narrow orbit and were blissfully unaware of the acute discomfort of the unfortunate dresser. I was the victim of this 'prank' on one occasion and was very thankful when the operation finished, as my legs were getting further and further apart in a desperate attempt to stop my trousers from coming down, and as I walked away from the table it was with difficulty I managed to hold them up. By this time the braces were far out of reach and the back two buttons could not be done up again.

Towards the end of the three months' appointment the Professor invited his dressers, together with his senior and junior house surgeons, to his house in the West End for what he called 'a sociable' evening, a change from our usual surgical chores. Although we were not to arrive until after dinner, nevertheless, we all dressed in dinner jackets, and as was really to be expected, the occasion proved to be rather an ordeal, at least it was as far as I was concerned. I believe we started with a glass of sherry or perhaps whisky, and later on the inevitable cup of coffee was handed round. I felt ill at ease, being still unsure of myself, and having little or nothing to add to the general conversation I felt sure the Professor would think I was a dull and most uninteresting person; I was certainly well out of my depth. After a while one of the House Surgeons was reluctantly persuaded to play the piano, and this quickly relaxed the tension - for in those far off days Professors were held in considerable awe by their students. Music, which has great soothing power, certainly relieved the atmosphere which, up to then, had consisted of polite but stilted conversation. After the pianist had finished, the Professor, in a lighter vein, said he was reminded of the man who very much enjoyed going to concerts of classical works, though he knew precious little of the technique; in the true sense he was not a musician. He had a friend however, who was very knowledgeable on this score, and as they usually went to musical performances together he naturally felt a little out of it, and did not wish to appear a complete ignoramus when it came to discussing how the work or works had been interpreted. One day he had an inspiration, and at the conclusion of the concert, as they were about to leave the hall, with a poker face and speaking in a tone of conviction remarked, "I felt that was a very moving performance, powerfully played, but 1 don't know what you think. I thought the conductor took liberties with the tempo in the second movement." One is left wondering if the friend fell for this musical acumen!

I think we were all glad when the time came to thank the Professor and his wife for a 'thoroughly enjoyable evening'. Shortly afterwards we were to move over to the medical side for the next three months. We still had however a further three months' surgery to do before sitting our finals.

Chapter Four

The medical wards were quite different from those I had just left on the surgical side, and the tempo was at a much slower pace, as the patients stayed in hospital much longer. With surgery you could see things really happening and could usually verify the correct diagnosis in the operating theatre. The patients, too, were more cheerful and enjoyed joking and talking about their operations. I was attached as a medical clerk to one of the last physicians of his day, for this Chief habitually wore a frock coat and was always immaculately turned out. Furthermore he would have nothing to do with fountain pens, when prescribing a drug, which he at all times wrote in Latin on a patient's chart, he would be handed a quill pen by the ward Sister, to be followed by a silver ink well presented to him by the senior nurse and lastly a sheet of clean blotting paper by a further nurse. It was an impressive and handsome way of prescribing and I am sure never failed to impress his patients, far more so than simply taking out a fountain pen from a pocket and writing the name of the drug in English. The patients were not, of course, supposed to see their charts, but I expect they did on the odd occasion when an opportunity arose.

Initially I found medical patients depressing - so many had been in hospital for lengthy periods, showing but little improvement. In those distant days the range of drugs was very limited, and many, if indeed not most of the diseases had to be left to run their natural course. At that time there was no specific treatment for pneumonia. All that could be done was pay attention to good nursing and to wait for the temperature to drop, hopefully suddenly, thus indicating the crisis. When this occurred recovery was to be anticipated. Many patients were not so fortunate, especially those past middle age, and before the discovery of Penicillin, pneumonia was called the 'Captain of the men of Death' and rightly so.

There were many other diseases besides pneumonia which at the time were often incurable, there being no known drugs to arrest the progress to a fatal outcome. As I write I can see so clearly the Chief, immaculate as ever, teaching at the bedside of a boy of twelve who had all the signs of tuberculous meningitis, a dreadful disease and always fatal in that era. I remember he asked one of the clerks how long he would expect the boy to live. Receiving no definite reply, the eminent physician held up the temperature chart which was ruled to last three weeks, and told us he would not require another one, it would more than last his time. I thought surely there must be some mistake for the patient did not look all that bad and I did so hope that on this occasion the Chief may, perhaps, after all, have been too pessimistic but unhappily this was not so, for death came well before the chart had expired. Now he could have been cured as, indeed, is the case with many other medical diseases, but in those days it was very different. No small wonder then that we used to say that few medical patients went home without a post mortem. This was really quite untrue but appealed to the students who thought the medical wards were gloomy whereas the surgical wards were just the opposite.

As I have said, my first medical clerkship was done on a firm which was still run on the lines of frock coats and quill pens, and we had to stand round the patients' beds whilst the great man discussed the cases in detail. With medical problems, this would be for what appeared at the time to be hours on end. My feet, at the conclusion of the ward round, which was never less than two hours and frequently longer, reminded me that prolonged standing was more tiring than walking for a similar stretch of time. One of the younger physicians was very popular as he used to teach that the secret of longevity was never to stand when you could sit, and never to sit when you could lie; and he practised what he preached by allowing his clerks to sit round the beds when discussing the cases.

As on the surgical wards, we were allocated our own cases to clerk and to examine. The pace was at a slower rate however, and the Chief, nearing the age of retirement, was more easy-going and was not a 'note tearer upper'. Despite his age he was an admirable teacher, and was great on aphorisms, his favourite being 'the commonest things are the commonest' and 'a living problem is better than a dead certainty'. This was typical of his straightforward and practical approach to a difficult differential diagnosis. On the rarest of occasions, despite the old world dress and courtly manner, he would unbend and even behave in a manner not really considered quite the thing by the sister in front of her nurses. An instance of this occurred when a student was asked the dose of a certain drug. Not really having any idea he made a wild guess, giving a ridiculously small amount. The Chief looked askance before remarking, "My dear boy, with that minute dose you might as well expect a fart to fertilise a field!" Loud laughter followed from all the clerks, but the sister, quite taken aback by this unexpected and what she considered uncalled for lapse of professional behaviour whilst on her ward, was far from amused. The poor nurses did their utmost not to giggle in front of sister's searching and disapproving eyes, but were hard put to it to restrain their mirth. In those days the ward sister reigned supreme, her word was law. As student clerks we were not allowed to speak to the nurses except through Sister, were only allowed on the wards at certain specific times, and if we dared to enter at any other time we would invariably be met with, "And who, may I ask, gave you permission to enter my ward?" She always seemed to be on duty, looking after her patients to the very utmost of her ability; a truly dedicated nurse, as indeed were all the sisters and nurses.

I was, by now, becoming more accustomed to seeing patients ill, often very ill, and at times distressed. But I had not as yet been present at an actual death, though a number had died both on the surgical and medical wards - as was only to be expected before the days of modern drugs more occurred on the medical side. When the end was thought to be not far away, screens would be placed around the bed, which had already been moved as near to the door as possible, so that when death finally came the body could be discreetly removed without upsetting the entire ward. All the same, the rest of the patients knew only too well what was happening and appreciated what the move to the end of the ward meant in the way of prognosis. At that time there were no side rooms or cubicles - just a main large ward.

From the screened bed could be heard the irregular and often laboured breathing, sometimes accompanied by groans and grunts of the expiring patient, seeming to go on for so long. At times, the respirations would cease momentarily only to start again, accompanied by a rattling sound - the well-named death rattle. Finally, all sounds would cease, and the relatives, who had remained at the bedside, would be gently led away by sister or nurse showing, as ever, wonderful compassion. We did not, as students, take any active part in these tragedies and were not allowed to go behind the screens. Nevertheless, I felt distressed whenever I knew there were loving relatives distraught with sorrow, sitting by the bedside of their dear ones, waiting for the inevitable end to come - it was all so tragic. I was to find, much later on, when as a surgeon I was actively involved, I was not to lose this feeling of intense compassion, and felt it even more acutely if the patient happened to be a child, and worse still, the only one of elderly parents.

Having completed the initial course of three months in each of the surgical and medical wards, before proceeding to further clinical subjects, we turned to the study of Pathology; a most important subject. Indeed, as the great physician William Osler was wont to say, 'as our pathology so is our medicine'. During this period we were required to assist at a stated number of post mortems, as well as to attend as many others as possible. The P.M. room was not nearly as dismal as the anatomy chamber where I had recently spent so many hours. Being lighter, it was more airy, and considerably cleaner, and had no partially dissected dead bodies lying around on odd tables. Neither was there the strong stench of carbolic - it was relatively spic and span. There were usually but two, at the most three, bodies lying naked on the clean whites cold slabs awaiting the arrival of the pathologist who was to perform the autopsy to verify the diagnosis. Or if none had been definitely made, to discover the answer which during life had eluded the doctors. The dead in the post mortem room differed from those awaiting anatomical dissections for they had ended their lives in the hospitals nearly always with close relatives by their side, had been lovingly cared for by the nurses over the final hours, and everything possible had been done to ease the passing, and now here they rested, so still and stiff and cold in all their nakedness. In these circumstances death seemed the more personal and so much closer. The preserved bodies of the dissecting room on the other hand, appeared that much more remote. No-one in the hospital had known them in life, still less in death, and they had been brought here for the sole purpose of teaching the doctors of the future, the last useful act they could perform.

Although the P.M. room did not smell of carbolic there was nevertheless a strong smell of disinfectants coupled with the sickly odour of death - difficult to describe, but quite characteristic. When I saw, for the first time, a lifeless body lying on a white slab for the final examination, it never crossed my mind that one day my own body would be similarly lifeless with all its functions stilled. I must have been too young, for in after years I have often thought along these lines.

When the pathologist arrived, he donned a long rubber apron together with rubber gloves, and assisted by a technician and student, he opened up the body and proceeded to demonstrate the relevant diseased lesions: the important organs being removed and placed on a separate slab for a more detailed examination. As the P. M. clerk, apart from assisting in a mild way, we had to try to unravel, and then to open the whole of the small intestine, some twenty two feet in all; and although I am not quite clear on this point, I believe we were not provided with gloves. I do remember however that it was a task I did not relish. The Professor, who was head of the department, normally put in an appearance, and after he had had a word with whoever was performing the autopsy, would proceed to discuss the findings, often picking up the appropriate specimen with his bare hands to emphasise the particular point. The first time I saw this I was amazed. To illustrate that pneumonia causes consolidation of the lung he proceeded to pick up a portion of lung tissue and to squeeze it between his fingers, expressing the typical frothy fluid exudate. Long before the days of antibiotics there was a risk attached to performing a post mortem if the case had died from septicaemia, and it was by no means unknown for even a small cut on a finger to prove fatal in such cases, and extra care was needed to make sure the knife did not slip. Obviously, the Professor must have known what he was about and was careful to avoid dangerously infected specimens, but we all thought it very odd that he chose to use his naked hands.

At the completion of the examination, the technician stitched up the long incision, so restoring the body to its former state. I was very surprised when I first saw how little such an extensive procedure had affected the appearance. The nearest relatives had always to give consent for a post mortem, and if they did not wish to do so, their wishes were, of course, strictly respected at all times. However, it was seldom that permission was not granted, for either they wished to know for certain the exact cause of death and to be reassured that nothing further could have been done to save their dear ones, or they felt the findings might help future patients as well as assisting in the training of 'the student doctors'.

Chapter Five

Following pathology, of which post mortems accounted for only a small part of the course, and before completing a final three months on a medical and surgical unit or firm, numerous other subjects had to be studied in various departments of the hospital. These included anaesthetics, gynaecology, and obstetrics, diseases of the ear, nose, and throat, of the eye, of skins, orthopaedics, fevers and so on: the list seemed almost endless. What an aspiring doctor had to know was truly daunting, and the thought of what had to be faced at the final examinations was undoubtedly frightening. Happily I was now becoming more, in fact much more, interested in medicine and was quite content to be a medical student; though I was still exceedingly inexperienced in worldly matters. Living so far away left no time for any social life with the other students. Not that I would have joined any societies anyway - I was still very much a loner. There was no question of a bar in the students' quarters, this was many years in the future, but quite a few used to go to a neighbouring pub where it was said the beer was excellent. Regrettably, in all my time I never once went. I still had a long way to go before I conformed to the norm!

Apart from anaesthetic and maternity appointments, which I will mention in more detail later, I cannot recall any strong impressions relating to the other departments which still remain in my mind. But I do remember being vaccinated before starting a course on fevers, and going to a hospital for infectious diseases, and being disappointed at not seeing a case of small pox, more especially as we had been vaccinated for this specific purpose! I have but a hazy recollection of what cases we saw, apart from erysipelas which in those days was a common and dangerous disease. Most often the face, head and neck were affected; the infected skin taking on a bright red colour, with an irregular edge which spread daily involving more and more of the previously healthy tissues. The first case I saw was in a bad way. The infection had already extended onto the forehead and closed the eyelids, with associated inflammatory swelling; the temperature was way up, and the patient was restless and showing signs of becoming delirious - all sure signs of advancing septicaemia. We were told that recovery was exceedingly unlikely and this prognosis proved to be correct, for on our next visit the patient was not there, having died as anticipated. At this period there were no known drugs which could be prescribed to arrest the relentless progress of erysipelas, or indeed any of the bacterial infections. One could only watch the patients and hope that their natural resistance would, with the usual supportive measures, overcome the toxaemia. Happily this is all now very much in the past.

I expect we must have been shown a variety of infectious diseases, but the only ones which I remember were those admitted with erysipelas, presumably because they presented such a striking clinical picture, and were often so very ill, and so little could be done in the way of adequate therapy. At the time I suppose I must have wondered if there was a risk of catching an infection on the visits to the fever hospital, but if I did it has left no lasting recollection. As a precaution we put on long gowns, caps and masks, and I do not imagine that we came into very close contact with the patients during the weeks of our fever course, we were not allowed into the wards at our hospital, for fear of introducing infection. Similarly, anyone associated with post mortems was not allowed to enter the maternity wards, as up to the advent of antibiotics, puerperal sepsis was a complication to be dreaded; so often it proved to be fatal.

Psychology, when I was a medical student, was in its infancy and was looked upon as rather a joke, and not taken seriously. As was to be expected, this new speciality attracted many comments, sometimes of an uncomplimentary nature. One of the kinder queries was to ask why the psychologist insisted on his wife sleeping under the bed, only to be informed that the reason was simple - he thought she was a little potty! Of our lectures on this subject I remember little apart from being told it was a dangerous practice to take on the attitude of self-pity, 'why should it always happen to me?' Self pity was to be avoided for it only led to depression. Instead, one should try to think of those worse off than 'poor little me'. Sound advice indeed but not always easy to follow, and in these days of high powered psychologists perhaps rather basic.

Of medical jurisprudence, or forensic medicine as it is now called, my mind is vacant as to what I learnt all those years ago. The only picture which remains is of various books being passed around the lecture room, so that we could take a look and decide which one we wished to buy, without exception they were all open at the same chapter: the one on rape! The class was large and when it came to my turn to view the books I saw that, whilst going the rounds, the most sexually explicit work had certainly been well fingered, and somebody had added in pencil, 'Confucius, he say, rape not very easy; a girl with her skirt up run faster than a man with his trousers down'.

Diseases of the ear, nose and throat and eyes were grouped together in a three months course. The removal of tonsils and adenoids was performed far more often at that time, and by modern standards was a relatively crude procedure. We, as students, alluded to it as the operation of spit-and-splash. The patients, usually quite young children, were put under an anaesthetic, and with an instrument known as a guillotine, the tonsils were manipulated into a snare-like aperture, and with a quick twist the operator pulled them out. When the remaining one had been similarly dealt with, the child was turned onto its side and the blood, which was by now usually flowing freely from the open mouth, was mopped away by means of a large sponge soaked in water. As by this time the patient was coming out of the anaesthetic and starting to splutter, it was quite often a bloody business - hence the term spit-and-splash. As students we could see next to nothing of the actual operation and looked upon these sessions as a waste of time.

The ophthalmic clinics were also not popular, and I was more or less at a loss, for the majority of the cases needed to be diagnosed by looking into the back of the eye with an instrument called an ophthalmoscope, which required considerable experience in its use. Once again I found the inability to keep one eye open and the other closed an added difficulty, and I doubt if I ever saw what I should have done. By rights, I should have been intensely interested in ophthalmology, as the correction of my short sight had made such a difference to my life, but I was pleased when the three months came to an end. I had found these specialities somewhat dull and uninteresting, and lacking the glamour associated with general surgery, and I looked upon my next appointment, which was to be anaesthetics, with relief.

As anaesthetic clerks we were attached in groups of three or four students to one of the visiting anaesthetic specialists, and were given instruction in the main operating theatre, as well as in the out-patient theatres, where minor operations were performed daily. Before the days of intravenous anaesthesia, and at the time I was a medical student in the late 1920's and early '30's, being 'put to sleep' as the patients called it, was at the best an unpleasant experience, and it could be a most nerve racking ordeal. It was small wonder the anaesthetic was more feared than the operation. Now, due to great advances over the years, no-one need have any fear - in place of acute apprehension has come complete reassurance, with a technique rendered so easy and so safe. Instead of an injection into a vein in the arm sending the patient off to sleep so pleasantly and naturally, the anaesthetist, with a few reassuring words, would place a mask over the face and commence to drop the anaesthetic, usually a mixture of chloroform and ether, onto the mask, the eyes being protected with a gauze square. The rate of drops was steadily increased until unconsciousness was induced, and the required depth of anaesthesia obtained. This was the ideal induction but by no means the rule, for ether is a very irritant vapour, and a fit, well built man could be a difficult subject to put under. The presence of a mask placed over the face, and the subsequent sensation of impending suffocation as the ether was poured on in ever increasing concentration, very naturally caused the patient to attempt to remove the offending mask with his hands; and when restrained, would struggle with all his might to free himself from this terrifying bondage. At this stage, a porter together with a nurse would have to restrain his body until unconsciousness was reached and the aggressive gestures stilled. On one occasion a hefty eighteen stone patient, a heavy beer drinker, managed to free himself and jumped off the trolley, half inebriated with the ether he had already inhaled, and made for the door.

Having successfully anaesthetised a patient, the art was to continue the anaesthetic in exactly the right quantity to allow the surgeon to perform the operation under the best possible conditions - too little and the patient would start to come round, too much and the respirations and heart would cease to function. As with everything else, it was a matter of experience. At first, as clerks, we only watched, but then came the time when we were to anaesthetise a patient ourselves, though closely supervised by the specialist. I must admit I was almost as nervous as the patient when it came to my turn. Fortunately the 'victim' had no idea that a student was on the job. I started off cautiously, too cautious indeed, for the patient seemed to be still awake in spite of my hesitant administration of the anaesthetic mixture on the gauze mask. The Chief told me quietly, to increase the flow of drops and not to get flustered. Eventually, with some further guidance, the patient lapsed into unconsciousness, and after an airway had been inserted in the mouth, we moved into the theatre ready for the start of the operation. Even now I can still sense how apprehensive I was throughout the operation. I had little idea how deeply anaesthetised my patient was. Would, at any moment, the surgeon angrily complain of the inadequate depth of anaesthesia, or on the other hand, would the respirations stop because I had overdone the amount of ether? The specialist kept a close eye on what was happening, though from time to time he would leave the theatre for a few minutes and I would be left on my own - I was then even more fearful. At long last the operation came to a close, and to my great relief all was safely over.

In those days, apart from the ordeal of going under, coming round from an anaesthetic was also an unpleasant sensation. Ether nearly always caused vomiting which often persisted for a considerable while, and if the abdomen had been opened, the pain produced by constant retching was acute. In addition the patients experienced a persistent taste and all pervading smell of ether.

Although we spent the majority of the time in the main operating theatres, we also did 'stuffing', as the anaesthetic appointment was called by the students, in the casualty and out-patient departments. Usually, this took the form of giving gas for incisions of septic fingers, boils and carbuncles, these being all too common in the pre-antibiotic days, and frequently leading to serious complications.

On one memorable occasion, I was detailed to administer gas to a robust, heavily built labourer, who had come to casualty with a septic finger. After the usual preliminaries, I placed a mask firmly over his face and turned on the gas valve. All proceeded according to plan initially, and I was beginning to think I had mastered the art of 'stuffing' with gas, when, quite suddenly, the patient stopped breathing, indicating either too much anaesthetic had been given and respirations arrested, or too little and consciousness was about to return. If the former, clearly no more gas must be administered - in my inexperience I felt there was no alternative but to remove the mask and reassess the situation. The out-patient room was noisy, so in order to hear the better and to ascertain if there was any evidence of normal respirations, I bent forward and applied my ear to the patient's mouth. At that very moment he woke up and emptied the entire contents of his obviously overloaded stomach slap bang in my face. I was literally smothered in vomit - it went up my nostrils, into my eyes and ears, all over my hair, even down my neck and chest, not to mention all over my pullover! I could barely see or breath, so heavy had been the deluge. I had peas up my nose and in my ears, and pieces of carrots, onions and the lot were enmeshed in my woolly pullover, which I was wearing at the time. The stench was appalling. The patient was, by now, wide awake and he had to be told to come back some hours later, with strict instructions not to have anything to eat or drink. He should not, of course, have been given an anaesthetic in the first place with a full stomach.

The nurses endeavoured to clean me up to the best of their ability, the woollen pullover proving especially difficult, and even after their valiant attempts I still stank of vomit, and was very conscious of this when travelling on the underground train that evening. The doctor in charge was not present at the time of this episode, but he must have been in the department for he told me afterwards that you learn a lot from your mistakes and quite often the hard way. Needless to say, my fellow students thought it all a huge joke, but took good care to keep well clear of my contaminated person.

Having completed the anaesthetic appointment I was beginning to feel I was developing into a real doctor. I had numerous dresserships and clerkships behind me, and had been through most of the departments, and the finals were not far away. I still had, however, to do mid-wifery and gynaecology, and to go out on the district for home deliveries, but this was not to be for another three months. First an orthopaedic appointment had to be completed. I must have found this subject rather dull, for it has left no lasting impressions.

Chapter Six

Christmas time was welcomed as providing a break in the routine of clinical studies, each firm of clerks and dressers being expected to put on a show to entertain the patients and staff. There was always great rivalry among the firms as to which one would produce the best performance, and each Chief took a great interest, expecting his students to give a good account of themselves. There was no question of opting out, all had to participate.

Preparations commenced some weeks before Christmas, and entailed being measured for the various costumes which were to be made by the nursing staff. What were considered 'delicate' measurements such as those for trousers, were left for ourselves to do with varying results for in those years strict modesty was the rule, and it would have been totally out of the question for a sister or a nurse to get within striking distance of the crutch.

Modesty was very much the order of the day and this even extended to the operating theatre. If an adult was on the list for a circumcision, all the nurses not actively involved in the operation, would be sent out by the theatre sister, it being considered improper for the young nurses to watch such procedures. When, on one occasion, the surgeon remarked to his students that he was reminded of the school boy's howler that, "Christopher Columbus was the first man to circumcise the globe with a fifteen-foot cutter!" Sister was decidedly not amused and considered it was in very poor taste.

To return to the ward Christmas shows: as was to be expected, it was by no means easy deciding on the content of the entertainment, especially as tradition decided that there must always be included topical skits and songs - and it was very difficult to know how far to go without giving offence to the senior members of the staff. Rehearsals, too, were difficult to arrange for more often than not, one or more members of the cast would not turn up in time. In actual fact, when the day arrived no-one was all that sure of their lines, so it was deemed essential, to help matters, to have a few preliminary drinks to oil the works. As each ward was visited, further topping-up measures were imbibed so that the last performance was somewhat unpredictable, and on one occasion the entire cast all but fell backwards off the makeshift stage!

The success of such impromptu shows depended to a large extent on the compere, who not infrequently had to extemporise at a moment's notice. Here, too, care had to be taken to avoid giving offence by the telling of risky stories - all too easy in the heat of the moment and in the welcome warmth of alcohol. Anecdotes of a medical or nursing content were always expected and never failed to gain loud applause.

Most of the ward shows were excellent, revealing remarkable and varied talents amongst the students. It was all good clean fun and was much appreciated by the staff and patients. The moral tone was inevitably of a high standard, and even such relatively innocent stories as the male patient saying to his nurse, "Come on, nurse, give us a kiss." And the nurse replying,

"No I can't, it's against the rules, I'm not even supposed to be in bed with you!" would have been considered beyond the pale in those days.

After the excitement of all the Christmas festivities we were soon back to our normal routine. Before starting on 'midder' there was a course on VD to attend. In those days it was known simply as the venereal diseases clinic, later on as the special treatment centre, still later as sexually transmitted diseases, and nowadays as Urogenital Medicine - the changing fashions in nomenclature. The sessions were held in a basement room, and in order not to reveal the patient's identity numbers were substituted for their names. Most of them looked rather sheepish and embarrassed and were not particularly helped to overcome this natural reaction by the specialist in charge. He was a large man, and very much down to earth, believing in calling a spade a spade and, if need be, a bloody shovel. He invariably wore a long gown and a pair of rubber gloves.

There were quite a few tales concerning this particular Chief and his department, which lost nothing in the telling, and may or may not have been true though they certainly had the ring of authenticity. He was reputed to have asked one of his VD patients what he was complaining of, and when told that he thought he had developed a cold in the end of his prick, the Chief took out his pocket watch, and holding it in his gloved hand, without more ado announced, "I give you three minutes to sneeze. If you haven't by then, it's Clap."

Another time, on being told by a patient that he had caught the infection from a public lavatory seat, he remarked, "That's a funny place to take a woman." His prize remark was when he told a male patient attending the clinic, "You put your person where I wouldn't dream of putting my umbrella."

In those days of long ago there were few drugs which had any specific action on venereal infections, and in consequence, the unfortunate patients had to continue to attend the clinics for considerable periods, and in some cases without the assurance of a complete cure; a marked contrast to the present time when modern drugs are so effective.

Writing of my student memories of the VD clinics I am reminded of the day when I stood in for the usual doctor at a provincial hospital special treatment centre. I had been qualified for a number of years, and the drug Penicillin had just become available for selected cases. It was still not in plentiful supply so was not routinely used.

A patient came into the clinic who was on the routine treatment of tablets, and who had shown little signs of improvement after a number of weeks. I explained that as the tablets were not clearing up the trouble, I would arrange for a short course of penicillin injections, which I felt sure would do the trick. This brought an immediate reaction from an obviously aggressive patient who replied, "I'm not having no bloody needles, whatever you say, doctor, I would rather keep on with the tablets." Thinking to reassure the belligerent gentleman, I said there was nothing to fear, that there was nothing to it, the injections were not painful and it was a perfectly straightforward procedure. To add weight to my reassurance I went on to say, "I can speak from my own experience as I have just finished a course of penicillin myself." Realising what I had said, I hastened to add, "for a septic finger!" Pointing to the injected digit I regret to say, despite my gallant efforts at persuasion, he still refused to have 'the needle'.

I have written only of males as patients of the special clinics, though of course females were also frequent attendees, coming on different days so the sexes should not be mixed.

Even at this comparatively late stage of my medical training I remained amazingly naive and was terrified of catching 'the bad disorders', and was determined not to put myself at risk. I had still to lose my virginity. The fear of VD had for me been intensified when I learned that one of my fellow students had been caught, and this reinforced my resolve not to take the slightest chance.

Chapter Seven

The practical part of our midwifery course lasted for six weeks and during this time we stayed in the hospital. We were expected to attend every confinement taking place in the labour wards for the first two weeks, in order to be shown the basic principles. The following four weeks we were to assist in deliveries in the patients' homes. This period was known as being 'on the district'.

Our living accommodation, even by the standards of those days, could only be described as spartan, and I can yet remember the extremely hard 'mattress' and the grim surroundings of the small and dismal room. I think we must have been called a great number of times those first couple of weeks, for the night porter invariably seemed to be knocking on the door in the early hours of the morning, announcing, "A case in the labour ward."

The drill was to dress as quickly as possible after this summons from a deep sleep, and to hasten across the quad to the maternity block. On arrival you had to scrub up before putting on the usual sterile gown, cap and mask, and only then were you allowed to enter the labour ward. As we were normally only sent for shortly before the actual birth was about to take place, if we did not make haste, there was the ever present risk of a B.B.A. - baby born before arrival, and this was the equivalent of a black mark against your name.

I shall never forget the first birth I witnessed and the disgust I experienced at what I deemed at the time to be a horrid and messy business, and what an unpleasant way of propagation for it all seemed so distasteful. Receiving a message that a patient was well on in labour, I hurried across to the maternity wards, and having scrubbed up and donned the usual garments, I entered the labour ward to be confronted by an excessively fat woman lying on her back with her massive thighs and equally large legs fully flexed at the hip and knee joints and suspended in stirrups. Had the patient been of a more normal build the sight would not have been so utterly repulsive, but under the circumstances it was far from a pleasant picture, and was made worse by the inevitable body odour which goes with so much fat. The young obstetrician who was in charge said he marvelled how the husband had managed to get his wife pregnant, she was so huge - he thought he must have put it in with a spoon!

By now the woman appeared to be well-advanced in labour, the pains were coming at regular and frequent intervals, and each contraction was accompanied by loud groans. She was constantly told to bear down and pull on a length of bandage which was attached to the end of the bed. The hair round the pubis, vulva and anus had been shaved prior to the onset, and now, as the pains came with ever increasing intensity, the lips of the vulva were seen to open and the head of the yet unborn baby to appear. With each contraction the head would descend a little further, but when the contractions ceased it appeared to regress, though in fact with each contraction further progress was made. Incongruously, I was reminded of an incoming tide, the waves waxing and waning, but eventually gaining their objective. At long last, following an extra strong contraction, accompanied with an extra loud cry, and a hard pull on the bandage, the head came out and the baby was born. The umbilical cord was quickly severed, and the infant handed to an experienced sister who was responsible for the immediate after care, it being vitally important that the lungs should be fully expanded and the baby not allowed to turn blue. It was not long before the placenta, or after birth was expelled accompanied by a rush of blood. The mother now appeared to be exhausted, but much relieved that all was safely over and she had a live, normal baby. I have been present at many births since those student days, but none have remained so clearly in my mind, for that first experience of labour made a strong and lasting impression on my still, and in some ways juvenile, approach to life, and I was indeed thankful that I had been born a man.

After seeing our first case, we assisted, on a rota basis, at all births occurring both by day and by night so that we could gain as much experience as possible before going out on the district, where all the cases would be normal, and most of which would already have had multiple pregnancies. The patients admitted to the hospital, on the other hand, were those whom it was considered needed special attention, as the labour was likely to be complicated for one reason or another. So long ago, there was no such thing as family planning, and most of the hospital clientele appeared to spend a large part of their lives getting pregnant. There was an old wives' tale that while the baby was sucking at the breast, further pregnancies would not happen, and for this reason, together with the economic factor, it was not unusual for mothers to continue to breast feed for well over the accepted period.

We discovered, when it came to deliveries on the district, conditions were far removed from those at the hospital. Here, the key note was one of quiet efficiency, the labour taking place under the best possible conditions with a highly trained staff constantly in attendance, and all the facilities readily at hand. Quite the opposite was the case when it came to home deliveries, for here, usually only the bare necessities were available, and sometimes not even these, and only too often in most unsuitable surroundings. The cases booked to have their babies at home had previously attended the ante-natal clinics and were considered to be 'normal' deliveries. Although we had only two weeks introduction to the process of childbirth, it had been very intensive, not to say hectic, and we were now considered ready to be put out on the district.

A strict rota was kept and when a patient started to go into labour, the hospital was informed, usually by the husband, and the student whose turn it was proceeded to the address, taking with him a large drum containing sterile gown, gloves, swabs, etceteras, together with the midder bag. As is so often the case with midwifery, many of the calls came at night, and although our district lay reasonably close to the hospital, some of the cases were a few miles distant, and at this time there was, of course, no public transport. In addition it frequently seemed to be raining. I cannot remember how my fellow students managed, though I believe there was a communal bicycle to be had. Houses reasonably near the hospital could be reached on foot, and as a last resort there was always a taxi, but as this had to be paid for by the students, few indeed could run to such opulence.

During our four weeks we were expected to get in twenty deliveries, and if the baby was a B.B.A. this was not counted. By far the vast majority had had several previous confinements, and as a consequence their labour was often quick. The difficulty was when sent for, we had no idea how much time we had to get to the house if it happened to be some distance and in the dead of night. At first, being new to the job, we tended to be over anxious for fear we should arrive when all was over. I was fortunate as I possessed a motor cycle which enabled me to lose little time in arriving at the house, but on looking back I do not know how I found the right address, for so often it would be in the early hours of the morning and I could not have known the district - furthermore there would be no-one about to ask. Possibly we were provided with an appropriate map but I do not know. I do remember, however, that on one occasion I took a very anxious father on the pillion of my motor-bike as he told me I would have great difficulty in locating the house at that time of night. He could not have had a very comfortable ride as I had to carry, in addition, a sterile drum as well as the usual midder bag. I think he must have sat on the steel drum whilst I wedged the bag on the petrol tank. I very soon learned that it was most unwise to leave my motor cycle outside in the street, as there was every likelihood of some part being stolen whilst I was busy with the patient. So I had to manipulate the fairly heavy and cumbersome bike through the narrow doorways and leave it in an equally narrow passage. At the time I owned a sports Levis twin stroke which possessed very wide handle bars which, more often than not, became impacted in the narrow door, much to my annoyance. On one occasion, being in a particular hurry, I did not stop to bother with this tiresome chore, and left it outside in the street. When I got to the patient and when she discovered I had not brought in my 'cycle' as she called it, I was advised to do so if ever I wanted to see it again.

The majority of the places we went to on the district were slums in the extreme, the sole accommodation in many instances being a single room in a large and dilapidated tenement block. The slightly better ones had part use of an old gas cooker situated in a passage outside; but usually the sole means of cooking was a single open gas ring in the room, and often a large and battered can the only supply of water. On entering, the 'compartment' would be dimly lit by an open gas mantle, the shabby curtains drawn across the window, even in the day time, so the neighbours opposite could not peer in; as a confinement, although all too common, never failed to cause speculations as to what was going on across the street.

The atmosphere was stale and generally unpleasant, and bugs were the rule and not the exception. I very soon discovered that the irritation resulting from their bites lasted for a considerable time, far longer than that from a flea, however hard I tried it was next to impossible to escape their attention. The turn-ups on a pair of trousers were a common place to find the little devils. On one occasion I left a note for the visiting midwife, and placed it amongst the glass covered bowl of artificial fruits and other knickknacks which so commonly adorned the mantelpieces. Some five minutes later, wishing to write an addition to the note, I found, what had only a short while ago been a sheet of clean paper, now contained six large and prosperous looking bugs, their bright colour showing up strikingly against the white background. Simple pressure was not enough to kill the little 'beggars', the trick was to crush them with a sharp edge. We used to see who could bring back the most bugs in a day. I cannot now be sure but I believe it was well into double figures.

The working of the district was very efficiently organised. The normal routine, when a confinement was on the way, would be for the midwife on duty to be called, together with the student whose turn it was on the rota. Unfortunately, in nearly every case the midwife would already have arrived and started to get organised before we came on the scene carrying the sterile drum and bag, and feeling more than a little uncertain of ourselves. The understanding ones, and taken as a whole they were almost without exception comprehending, would say to the patient "here comes the doctor to help us now there will be nothing to worry about" and would continue to address us as 'Doctor', a wonderful and most welcome uplift to our morale. They would then proceed to show us what to do, but in such a tactful manner that we felt we were doing it ourselves, and every now and then would let drop the magic word 'Doctor'.

The district midwives were, almost without exception, highly competent and experienced nurses. Undoubtedly, without their skill and help, we would have been, in many cases, at a loss. As it was, by tactful suggestions to the young 'Doctor', the labour usually came off without any undue incidents. If we were uncertain, or more accurately, if the midwife was not satisfied with the progress being made, there was always an obstetrical house surgeon on call and he would come out immediately. Not for him the hospital bicycle but in the luxury of a taxi cab. As I have mentioned, almost always when we received a call to a patient thought to be in labour, by the time we arrived at the 'house' everything was taken care of by the midwife, who, having attended so many births over the years, knew just what to do and when to do it. I suspect the call went to the nurse some time before we were informed at the hospital, thus ensuring that we would not find ourselves the first arrival on the scene without the necessary skilled assistance on which we relied to a considerable extent.

On one occasion this happy arrangement was not to be. It was evening time and I was first on call on the rota when the porter told me that there was a case starting in labour at such-and-such an address and I had 'best get cracking'. I duly collected the sterile drum and midder bag and set off on my motor cycle, quietly confident, as I had been on the district now for more than two weeks, and felt I was beginning to get the hang of bringing new born babies into the world - there didn't really seem to be all that much to it. The mother did all the work, and anyway there was always the midwife in attendance. What was required was calm confidence combined with reassurance from the attending nurse and doctor. On arrival at the house however, it could really hardly be called a house, being just one room in a slum tenement I was dismayed to find that the midwife had not yet put in an appearance, and for the first time I was on my own without her invaluable support.

The patient greeted me with relief, exclaiming, "I'm glad you've come, Doctor." (That magic word, how sweetly it sounded, though I felt at this stage, far from being a doctor, and fervently wished the midwife would arrive.) "The pains started after I 'ad 'ad me tea, and now they are becoming that keen." The patient's mother, who was fussing about in the room told me with pride that her daughter had been ever-such-a-good-girl and had been married for a full three months and it was her first baby! A neighbour, a kind of Sarah Gamp, was also in attendance, and professed to know all there was to know about confinements and gave the impression that as she was there, the presence of a midwife or doctor was quite superfluous, a view which when I drew close to her she certainly held on washing. The room was, as usual, sparsely furnished and poorly lit with a single gas jet and even though it was still light outside, the curtains, possibly at one time a pleasant pastel shade but now dingy with grime, were drawn across the one small window in order to stop peeping Toms peering in from across the street.

Having arrived on the scene unexpectedly and unfortunately, first, I felt I must do something rather than hang about waiting for the midwife, especially as I was being addressed as 'Doctor', and it was quite plain that some action was expected. I therefore proceeded to put the normal routine into operation. I asked for a kettle to be put on to boil the water coming from a can under the bed. As it was a rule to administer an enema prior to a birth, in the absence of a nurse and although part of her normal duties, I considered I had no alternative but to proceed; we had as students been instructed as to the technique though I had never given one. Trying hard to convey the impression that this was to me almost a daily occurrence, I took from my bag a lump of soft soap and carefully taking from it a piece approximately the size of a walnut, proceeded to dissolve this in a pint of water. Having done so, I then inserted the soapy solution into the patient's rectum and lower bowel, using a Higginson's syringe which was part of our equipment. There was no available bed pan or chamber pot for her to use, the only receptacle being a bucket, the rim of which was anything but smooth. Indeed, the rough edges must have been most uncomfortable, but the patients on the district apparently always took the lack of refinements as a matter of course, and hardly ever complained.

At this stage I felt quite pleased with myself and was sure the midwife would be suitably impressed when she came, probably full of apologies for not having arrived sooner - but she didn't come. As the labour pains were continuing with what appeared to be increasing frequency, I deemed it expedient to put on my sterile gown and gloves, and to get ready to deliver the infant, though still hoping that the nurse would be in time for the actual birth. I accordingly scrubbed my hands and fore-arms as best I could, using a cracked enamel basin so very different from the porcelain sinks with their plentiful supply of hot running water back at the hospital, and, putting on the sterile cap, gown and mask and sterile gloves, I instructed the two women in the room to turn the mother to be on her left side and to make her as comfortable as possible. I had now reached the point of no return as I had put on the only sterile gown and gloves which we routinely carried. The voluntary hospitals had constantly to consider every penny spent and could not afford to issue duplicate sets, especially to medical students. I was thus now unable to touch anything not already sterile. I was all prepared to conduct the delivery under the best possible aseptic conditions, puerperal sepsis at that time being a most dangerous complication and one to be avoided at all costs.

I managed as best 1 could to get everything arranged according to the book; the patient, in the meantime had settled down on her left side, but continued to complain of intermitting griping pains. Placing sterile towels around the perineum and holding a sterile pad over the anus in the approved manner, I awaited the advent of the baby's head arriving at the vagina; there was still no midwife and I was now becoming reconciled to carrying out the delivery entirely on my own, my first solo flight into midwifery, so to speak! After I had been in this cramped and unnatural position for some time, unable to move as one hand was holding the precious sterile pad over the patient's rectum, I began to feel unbearably warm. The room was small and airless, and a hissing gas jet, although giving but slender illumination, nevertheless contributed in no small way to the general fetid atmosphere. The pains now began to lessen in intensity and to come at longer and less regular intervals. The Sarah Gamp said that what was wanted to hurry up matters was a nice hot strong cup of sweet tea which she proceeded to brew. I cannot recall how the sole supply of water, which was kept in a can, was replenished, but presumably from a tap somewhere in the outside passage. When the tea was mashed, a cup was poured out for the young doctor who was being 'ever so kind'. I had the greatest difficulty in explaining that I could not touch anything unsterile, and had to brush aside the remark that 'a nice cuppa never did nobody no 'arm, and the crock's been washed since being used at dinner time'. All the same I would have appreciated a drink; being hot and thirsty, and unsure what to do next as the course of the labour was not advancing as expected. By this time I had resigned myself to accepting the fact that there would be no midwife to advise or help. I did not feel justified in calling out the house surgeon from the hospital as clearly the patient was in no danger. The trouble appeared to be, to my inexperienced eyes, merely an unduly prolonged labour.

Although it is over fifty-five years since I found myself gowned and gloved in that tenement room, the memory is as clear as though it were yesterday. I recall, as the night drew on, the atmosphere grew almost unbearably stuffy, and I became damp with sweat and anxiety, and longed for a cool drink. In addition, I had developed severe cramp, being forced to remain immobile for so long in such an uncomfortable and unnatural position. I virtually could hardly move as I still conscientiously held on to the sterile pad. I continued to be offered copious cups of tea - the reason I could not become unsterile had not been accepted - and I would have given almost anything for a drink. The sight of the others enjoying what was said to be a lovely refreshing cup did nothing to slake my thirst. I was too worried to feel any desire for food, my one desire was to deliver a live baby. The long night drew slowly to a close, and at last, through a chink in the drawn curtains, a glimpse of the dawn appeared.

After all those endless hours and seemingly with no actual progress being made with the delivery, I sensed a definite air of mistrust creeping towards the young doctor - I must admit with good reason. The mother of my patient may well have suspected that I was a mere student for she now wondered if, perhaps, I should call in another 'Doctor'. She stressed the word 'another' which I thought was tactful of her. However, as her daughter continued to be clinically fit, I decided to wait a few hours before sending for help, as it was still only early morning. The labour pains had lessened considerably by now and were coming at only infrequent intervals; there was still no sign of any stretching of the perineum, and even less sign of a head appearing. Even with my very limited experience I sensed that the confinement had reached a standstill! Looking back, I need not, of course, have remained gowned and gloved, and in a position of considerable discomfort for all these long hours, and I am sure, too, that the expectant mother must have been thoroughly browned off lying in one position throughout the night, with a young man's hand firmly clamped on her backside! But at that time, due to inexperience, coupled with anxiety at having to make decisions on my own, I felt I was only doing my duty to the best of my ability, and was simply attempting to carry out to the letter all that we had been taught. When the dawn gave way to full daylight, and the sounds of the morning traffic began to filter into what was by now the almost unbearable heat and fug of the cluttered-up room, I at last came to the conclusion that there was no future in continuing this vigil any longer, and as I was clearly getting out of my depth, the time had come to seek help. So without more ado I sent a message to the hospital asking for assistance. Although, at first, I had been welcome as the doctor who had come to deliver the baby, as the hours dragged on, the attitude towards me had shown a steady and justifiable deterioration. The Sarah Gamp, towards the end of the night, had as good as said that I wasn't doing things right, if she were in charge she would 'have the little bugger out in next to no time!'

The patient's mother, on the other hand, was too concerned for her daughter's safety for any open criticism of my obstetric powers, though I expect she had grave doubts as to my experience. Having sent for help I continued to remain in my sterile garb and in my cramped position right to the moment when the house Surgeon arrived. I wanted to give the impression I was really doing my stuff in the approved manner - no slip shod methods for me when it came to conducting a confinement, even without the help of a midwife. But alas, all my efforts were wasted for it took the H.S. next to no time to inform me in no uncertain terms that I had been a silly B.F., as the patient was not in true labour - she had merely experienced false pains, and in all probability would not have her baby for a week or even longer. He was correct in this for the birth took place just two weeks later, though needless to say I was not this time in attendance. The house surgeon was very far from pleased at being called out before he had had his breakfast to a case that was not even in labour. For my part, I felt crestfallen as I gathered up my belongings and said farewell to the room where, only twelve hours before, I had entered with such high hopes for a successful delivery, only in the end to make such a fool of myself. I have no doubt the Sarah Gamp would be delighted that her opinion of me had been truly vindicated! I never discovered why the midwife failed to turn up. It was most unusual for any slip-up to occur, as the organisation was very efficient - presumably on this rare occasion the message must not have been sent.

My exploits soon got around and were hugely enjoyed by my fellow midder students. Happily, the remainder of the twenty cases which I was required to attend went without any further incidents, no doubt largely due to the presence of the midwife.

In addition to participating in the confinement, we had to visit the patients daily to take the temperature, to see that the discharge from the uterus was running a normal course, and to keep an eye on the new born infant. These visits seldom coincided with those of the nurse who also paid daily visits, hers being the ones that really counted, for we were still very much the learners. The experience, apart from the obstetric side, was very valuable as it enabled us to see for ourselves the conditions under which the patients lived; all so very different from what we saw in the clean surroundings of the wards. The environment was utterly different and it served to give an insight into the problems and difficulties of domicilliary medicine and in addition to teach the rudiments of being an understanding and sympathetic doctor.

I found a motor cycle a very great help when working on the district, as it made visiting easy, and after several hours of attending a labour, it was a most welcome change to feel the cool fresh air rushing past my face, after breathing the hot fetid atmosphere of the room, and being in close contact with the all pervading odour of stale bodies. It was also soothing to feel the power of the engine and to hear the regular purr of the twin exhausts. I was at that time an enthusiastic motor cyclist.

It was a long established tradition, having completed our midder cases, on our last evening of our residence in the hospital, to throw a party and invite the junior obstetricians who had been responsible for our somewhat amateur efforts whilst on the district. It was an 'all male' affair; the days when women would be allowed were many years distant. The usual barrel of beer was ordered which would, in due course, be drunk to the last drop. I was, by now, gaining considerably more confidence in myself, though I still had some way to go before I felt in full harmony with the behaviour of my fellow students. For one thing, I really didn't like the taste of beer and consequently drank little, and had no wish to participate in what was commonly called a 'bloody good piss up' which took place from time to time. On this occasion I certainly drank the least.

As the evening wore on and the level of the beer steadily fell, someone had the bright idea that we should all recount our most amusing or exciting incident whilst working on the district, or failing this, tell a story with a definite midder content. This suggestion was immediately accepted with universal approval, and it was duly agreed that no-one would be excused - any defaulter would be in for a de-bagging. When it came to my turn I didn't feel inclined to recount the occasion when I had made such a fool of myself on the night of the false labour, and not having had any other experience worth repeating, I decided to relate an incident which I believed to be authentic. This concerned a down-to-earth lady, well versed in the art of motherhood, who was attempting to breast feed her baby whilst riding on a tram. In those days the passengers sat facing each other on long benches which stretched the length of the car. Her blouse was open to expose the full breasts, but despite repeated attempts, she just could not get the baby to suck, and at last, in desperation, announced in a loud voice to the crowded tram, "If you don't want the breast, you little bugger, I will give it to the gentleman beside me!" This episode as I recounted it, met with approval, though most had doubts as to its authenticity. After further stories and anecdotes, the beer and the party came to an end more or less at the same time, and my midder experience as a student to a close.

I had enjoyed the weeks and had learned many things apart from obstetrics. As I left the residency I gave one last, almost nostalgic, glance at the notice board which we had consulted each morning to find our place on the rota. In place of the usual list, some wag had written,

> Simple Simon, simple soul,
> Bought a book on birth control;
> But judging by his wife's condition
> He must have bought the wrong edition.

Chapter Eight

The final examinations were close. The supreme ordeal was now to be faced after nearly six years of intensive training and studies, and on the result rested the all-important question whether I would, at long last, be able to write Doctor before my name. When I had started as a young and exceptionally naive medical student, at that time, uncertain if I really wanted, or indeed could, actually manage to become a doctor, the final exams had seemed to be so far into the future as to be almost unattainable. Even the clinical years, when white coats and stethoscopes marked the advancement to the wards from the lecture rooms, appeared well into the future. And now, all this was behind me and the fulfilment of all those years of hard work was within my grasp. It only remained to satisfy the examiners that I was a fit person to be let loose on the public as a fully qualified doctor. I was, by this time, very in tune with a medical career, and keen to have the opportunity of putting into practice all that I had been taught.

The day to sit for the written papers dawned at last. Catching an early train up to town so as to be sure to arrive in good time, on the hour's journey I had ample opportunity to think of all the questions I might well not be able to answer, but I made no attempt at a last minute revision at this critical stage I found that the more I read the less I seemed to know. I had come to the conclusion that the best practice was to work hard till the day before the examination, and then to shut all the books, and go into the examination room fresh, having spent the previous day at leisure, though inwardly tensed up at the thought of the morrow. I arrived, as did many others, too early at the examination hall, and had to stand around hoping that the papers would be reasonably straightforward. At last, and it seemed such a long at last, the double doors were thrown open and we trooped in to our allotted desks. Then came the ordeal of waiting for the presiding examiner to place the paper before me. I watched as those in front received theirs and tried to discern from their expressions if the questions set were difficult, but I could see no signs of either relief or dismay. When it came to my turn, as the paper fell I glanced quickly down and was relieved to find the questions were straightforward and

I thought I could manage to write reasonable answers. We wrote in books, and if required, extra pages could be obtained. There were always a few who would fill the books and ask for additional loose leaves, on hearing such a request I felt envious, for clearly, those candidates must know far more than I did to use so many pages for their answers, whereas I myself would not even fill the book. To my anxious eyes they looked so smug getting up for a further supply, giving the impression that they knew it all and there wasn't room to get it all down.

I have read, in books, of examinees, only too well aware of the chance of a failure, taking cribs into the examination, possibly using very small print on the shirt cuffs, etc., and asking to be excused to visit the lavatory; a request only granted on the understanding that an attendant accompanied the candidate to wait outside the loo. Even though the time spent inside had obviously to be strictly limited, there would be an opportunity to glance at certain cribs secreted on the body. Be that as it may, in my personal experience of a large number of exams, I saw no evidence of this practice, and all were conducted in a perfectly fair and straightforward manner, and I very much doubt the authenticity of this suggestion.

It was usual, after we had written a paper, to compare notes in an attempt to assess how well we had answered the various questions. Almost invariably, some bright spark would ask if we had remembered to list an important differential diagnosis. If we had not, we would be more than a little disturbed, for what had up to then been considered a reasonable paper, now appeared more in doubt. I eventually came to the conclusion that it was better, and less nerve racking, not to hold a post mortem with other candidates, for it only served to increase the worry of the possibility of failure.

Whereas the written papers of the finals were bad enough, the practicals and vivas were a much worse ordeal. It was a time of acute apprehension whilst waiting in the antechamber before being called by a uniformed porter into the examination hall, and being directed to a green baize table where two examiners were seated ready to decide your future. It was considered essential, as a potential doctor, to be well dressed and dark suits were the order of the day. Students of the last century were even expected to attend their final oral examinations dressed in the formal morning clothes of that time - failure to observe this convention was to court disaster, as one candidate was to discover. Thinking he could well have failed, having written poor papers, he considered it was really not worth while to take the trouble to 'dress up' and accordingly presented himself wearing an ordinary tweed suit. His examiner, a noted Edinburgh physician of his day, resplendent in an immaculate morning coat and striped trousers, took but one look at the candidate before ringing for the janitor. When he arrived, he was requested, "To show this gentleman to the golf course!" In those far-off times great emphasis was placed on professional conduct of a high order, and the slightest lapse was totally abhorred.

In addition to the written papers and vivas, an important part of the finals was the examination of various cases and the arrival at their correct diagnosis. By far the majority of the patients, brought in specially for the purpose, were co-operative, but the occasional one could be truculent. It was my misfortune to be taken by the examiner to such a patient and told I had twenty minutes to carry out a full examination and to make a diagnosis. From the very outset I was met with open hostility, and found it next to impossible to obtain a clear history, an all important aspect of the diagnosis. When I asked what was the matter he replied, "That's what you're 'ere for to find out, if you're to pass this 'ere medical exam. It wouldn't do for me to tell you." I tried to explain that I was merely enquiring about his symptoms and how long he had had the pains. He replied by saying, "a tidy while." When I again enquired what he meant by a tidy while - was it a matter of years, months or weeks, he answered, "I dare say it would be." I was by this time, feeling pretty desperate as the minutes were fast ticking away and so far I had got nowhere. In one last attempt I said, "Do please tell me how long you have had the pains, it is so important for me to know."

"How long have I 'ad the pain?" he repeated. "Why ever since it started of course."

Even though my history taking had been a fiasco, I felt I must carry out the usual routine examination with the hope that I might be able to salvage the situation. But here again I met with obstruction. I was told to 'take your hands off my stomach, they're bloody cold!' and he went on to complain he hadn't consented to attend the examination hall to be mauled about mere students; he had been led to understand he would be up for diagnosis by proper doctors.

I was now in a sweat. It was absolutely essential to do well in the long case if I was to pass, but when the examiner came at the end of the twenty minutes to ask about my findings and provisional diagnosis, I would be in no position to answer and could only expect to fail. Realising that the situation was rapidly becoming desperate, I took my courage in both hands, left the well nigh impossible patient, and with trepidation approached one of the examiners to explain my predicament. At first he thought this was just a ruse on my part to get out of a long case which I found I was unable to diagnose and knew next to nothing about. However, he came back with me to the uncooperative man, and I was relieved and delighted when the eminent examiner faired little better than the humble examinee, being met with downright rudeness. I was told I had been quite correct in complaining and was sent off to another case, with suitable apologies, and an assurance that my first patient would never be asked again.

The cases selected for examination purposes came from the various teaching hospitals, and almost without exception were helpful and kindly to the young 'doctors', fully appreciating their ordeal. On one occasion a patient told me to be sure to palpate a particular area of the abdomen, because the gentleman examiner is bound to ask, and 'if you haven't done it right, 'e doesn't 'alf blow off'. A number of the chronic cases had been coming up to the examination hall for a number of years, and looked upon the occasion as a pleasant outing with a modest payment for their services at the end of the day.

Although our long case was the most important to get right, we had, in addition, a number of what were called short cases to diagnose. The examiner would conduct the candidate to selected patients and ask, "Now what do you make of that?" pointing to a lump, or, "What is your diagnosis?" or again, "What treatment would you advise here?" The majority appreciated the candidates' nervousness and accordingly made allowances, though there was the odd one who had a bad reputation for being bluff and quick tempered, with an overbearing manner. However, despite their, at times, terrifying attitude of conveying to the poor examinee that he was a perfect idiot, they compensated by being lenient with their marks. The examiner, on the other hand, who was smooth and polite and said very little might well be marking the candidate down. Again it was my luck to meet one of the blustering and impatient kind whom everyone fervently hoped to escape. I was asked to mark out a blood vessel on a patient's leg and was handed a pencil. True to form, before I really had time to think where to place the mark, I was told to get on with it, and not to stand around like a blithering idiot waving the pencil in the air - surely I knew what a pencil was for? But he passed me and all was forgiven!

When the day arrived for my final viva I was more than ever anxious not to make a mess of it, as I considered that I had done reasonably well up to now, and was not conscious of having dropped any major bricks. All went surprisingly smoothly until towards the end, when I was asked about a particular disease of which I knew next to nothing. The kindly examiner, and I shall never forget his wonderful words, told me, on reaching home that evening, 'as a doctor', to look the subject up in my text book. I left the room with a sense of enormous relief, but later began to think perhaps I had read into his words more than was intended, especially as I had been unable to answer that particular question, and the more I thought about it the less certain I became.

In those far off days candidates were not notified through the post if they had passed or failed. Instead, they were required to attend at the examination hall at 6.15 p.m. punctually, in the evening following the completion of the vivas, to be informed personally of the results. Candidates who had finished their exams that day, assembled in an anteroom to await their fate. After what, at the time, seemed like hours of acute anxiety, a porter appeared and began to read out the examination numbers. Each would then go up in turn to a resplendently attired attendant, who, having verified the number as correct, and this, to the waiting and would be doctor, appeared to take an age, would announce 'passed' or 'failed'. Failures were handed a pink form, giving particulars of when the examination could be taken again, and were shown out through the 'failed' door. Those who had passed proceeded through another door to a large and imposing room where the examiners were assembled in full regalia. After the customary congratulatory remarks, the newly qualified doctor swore to observe the Hippocratic Oath - an impressive and memorable occasion. It was indeed a marvellous feeling to have accomplished the goal which initially appeared to be so far ahead and beset with so many hurdles to overcome. The ordeal of waiting for the porter to call out my number is still with me. I remember seeing the preceding candidates going through either the passed or failed doors, and wondering which one was for me; and when, after what seemed to be an eternity, I heard my number, I stepped forward, steeling myself to face up to the result, and what a wonderful relief to hear that magic word 'pass'!

This system, which was really almost bordering on the cruel, has long since been discontinued. It was, without any doubt, an unkind way of announcing success or failure but in my day, medical students were expected to be tough and well able to cope with such tense situations. There was no nonsense of having to be put on tranquillisers before taking exams, and no question of running off to psychologists if unable to face up to the stresses and strains of student life.

It was a very fine feeling to be a doctor, and a welcome and much needed boost for my morale, for despite my dismal start in life, with a grave speaking defect, neglected defective vision, and subsequent miserable school days, I had at last achieved success, and moreover, I was now quite sure I would be happy living the life of a doctor. It was good to know all those years of hard work had been so much worth while. I have nothing but praise for the medical school and have been everlastingly grateful for all that it did for me. I arrived excruciatingly shy and awkward, not to mention gauche, and was extremely unsure of myself. But as the years passed I gradually overcame these difficulties, and by the time I qualified, although still some way to go, I was well on the way to becoming an average person. Without any doubt, the time I spent at my splendid medical school proved to be the making of me. I was, at all times, treated with consideration and came into contact with many fine people. I have happy memories of those days, all so very different from my wretched school experiences.

From the start of our medical training we were taught always to remember to put ourselves in the place of our patients, and also to remember that medicine was a 'calling' and not a 'trade'. The patients, for their part, were very kindly treated; and although the discipline was strict, it was a happy hospital, and we, as students, were continually reminded that the most important person to be considered must always be the patient. It was with mixed feelings that I walked through the archway for the last time - it seemed an age since I had called the head porter 'Sir' on the morning of my arrival.

Chapter Nine

My parents were naturally pleased that I had passed my finals, though I suspect my father was secretly disappointed that I had not graduated from Edinburgh, his old Alma Mater. Eighteen months before I qualified he had suffered a severe heart attack, which had caused him to retire, the house being sold with the practice as was the usual custom at that time. This meant that I could no longer look forward to taking over the practice which had been the original idea ever since I had been 'sent' to do medicine. My Father had tried to keep the practice on until I could qualify, by employing an assistant, but it was not a very satisfactory arrangement, and in the end it had to go. I suppose I must have been disappointed at the time, but looking back, it was probably a good thing, for the young and the old (my Father was 70 years old at the time) do not usually see eye-to-eye. I now had no definite plans for the future. I felt however, before deciding on the next move, that I had earned a short holiday, and accordingly set off with my brother in his little car - one of the first baby Austin's - to the New Forest. The few days we spent there were heavenly, it was just too good to be true. I lost no opportunity of letting it be known that I was a doctor, and got great satisfaction when signing the hotel register, the very first time 1 had occasion to write Dr. on an official form - it gave me a fine feeling and it looked good. I have not forgotten the euphoria of that holiday. Nor have I forgotten the cat that did its 'refusals' in one of my shoes which I had left outside the bedroom door for the night porter to clean; the accepted practice at that time. For reasons best known to the cat, he or she decided a shoe was a convenient and suitable 'earth box' and with commendable accuracy had contrived to empty its load full tilt into the inside of my shoe. I thought at the time, if only the cat had realised that this shoe belonged to a fully qualified doctor, he might have shown more respect for my so recently acquired status and taken care to go elsewhere to leave such a nauseating mess.

The holiday over, the future had to be faced. It was certainly great to be a doctor but what to do next was a difficult decision to make. When I qualified, and for many years after, it was not necessary to spend any time doing junior hospital appointments before full registration. Despite the lack of practical experience, it was quite in order to go into general practice immediately after graduation, as indeed many doctors did. I decided, however, that I should aim to spend at least a year doing hospital jobs, as I realised only too clearly how inadequate I was in many ways when it came to practical experience, and I felt I owed this to future patients. I had already made up my mind to try to become a really good doctor even at this early stage of my medical career, and I think I appreciated the great responsibility which would remain throughout my working life. The question was, how and where to obtain my first appointment as a house surgeon or house physician. It was no use to think of applying to my teaching hospital where the competition was fierce in the extreme, and where in those days appointments largely depended on two achievements; the one, and more valuable, was to be a member of the first XV Rugby team, for great importance was always attached to winning the inter-hospital Rugby cup, and every effort was made to retain the good players. The other was to have been outstanding in the examination results, preferably winning a prize. Having no claim to either of these desirable assets, I considered it pointless to apply for a job 'on the house' as it was called. There were those however, who, despite not being in the first XV or having shown outstanding brilliance as students, were determined to get appointed to their teaching hospital, and usually succeeded, though it could well mean hanging around for a considerable time. These appointments were regarded almost as an honour, and I think I am correct in saying, carried no salary, though being resident in the hospital, the keep was free. The hours worked were long and more often than not arduous in the extreme. The kudos of working for Harley Street specialists was considered to be ample reward; only a relatively few were fortunate to obtain such posts, the majority had to apply elsewhere.

It so happened that a vacancy occurred at this time at the local hospital and, as my Father had for many years been in practice in the nearby village, I thought it was worth while sending in an application. In due course I was requested to attend for an interview, and was offered the post of junior house surgeon at a salary of £80 p.a. plus board. In those days, obtaining the first post after qualification, having no experience, was not easy, and I was greatly relieved to have succeeded at my first try - doubtless, being a local boy was a great help. The hospital had but two resident doctors - the other house surgeon was senior to me, and received the princely sum of £120 p.a.

Although the building was quite modern, with extensive grounds surrounding it on all sides, the actual management of the hospital was reminiscent of the Victorian era. Attempted suicides were strictly barred from its doors; such cases had to go to the work house where surgical facilities were almost non-existent. In those days it was considered wicked to attempt to take ones own life, and if unsuccessful, on no account were they to be admitted to the general hospital. Late one night, long before my Father retired, he was called out urgently to an outlying farm where he found the owner to be bleeding profusely from a self-inflicted gaping wound in the neck. It was abundantly clear that unless he was admitted to hospital as a matter of great urgency, he would certainly die. Without further ado, my Father put him in the car and rushed to the hospital, and against the strict rule, deposited his patient in the casualty room. Once there, he had to be admitted. Had he been sent to the work house he would certainly have died. The Board of Governors were extremely displeased at this most irregular way of bringing a patient to the casualty department, and very much against the strict rules. A special meeting was called and a strong letter of protest sent to my Father. I believe his only concern was for the patient who, happily, survived though perhaps a little concerned that his suit was covered all over with blood, not to mention the car upholstery being in the same state.

In the early 1930's hospitals, apart from the few municipal ones, were entirely dependent on the voluntary contributions and fund raising activities of various kinds. In the hospital about which I am writing, it was the custom for those of independent means to donate annually a substantial sum, and in return to be given what were known as letters of recommendation. On being admitted, patients had to bring with them one of these letters. If the admission was an emergency, then the letter would have to be produced subsequently, for it was a necessary requisite. Obtaining these letters could at times be a tiresome chore. It entailed going to the house of a benefactor to ask for an introductory letter. It might be that this person had none left, in which case, a second or even a third benefactor would have to be visited before the precious bit of paper could be obtained. Not until then would the hospital authorities be satisfied. Needless to say, the quantity of letters of recommendation each benefactor received for the distribution depended on the size of the yearly donation. There was no doubt that in those days, hospitals were invariably short of money, and every penny spent had first to be carefully considered, and although this routine was a way of raising money, it put the patients or their close relatives to a lot of unnecessary trouble; undoubtedly they had more than enough worries and anxieties without the additional chore of having to collect a letter from a benefactor, a system which now seems archaic to say the least.

There were only two figures who really counted in the hospital hierarchy - the Matron, Miss Agnes Andrews, and the Chairman-cum-Secretary, Mr. Bardell Barton; a landed gentleman who gave freely of his services without thought of remuneration, and dearly loved the hospital. He was instrumental in raising large amounts of money, and spent the greater part of every day working in his office. Mr. Barton liked to look upon the occupants of the wards, not so much as patients, but as guests for the duration of their illness. This struck me as being a very human approach, though I fear it was not always put into practice. The autocratic Miss Agnes Andrews had been in her post for many years and literally ran the hospital; she was hand in glove, as the saying goes, with the chairman, and he usually did as she wanted. Miss Andrews was very definitely a matron of the old school. Then well past middle age, she had failed to move with the times, and the standard of discipline she demanded from the nurses was far and away too strict. She wielded far too much power - and her word was law, and above all she showed a complete lack of understanding when dealing with the problems that a matron had to face.

It was the accepted custom in all operating theatres for the surgeons to break off some time between cases for a refreshing cup of tea, a most welcome and often necessary respite after a long and taxing operation. Miss Andrews however, did not agree with this and would not allow the theatre staff or the kitchen to supply either tea or coffee - she said the surgeons were there to operate and not to stand around drinking tea! The result was that they brought their own tea in thermos flasks. It still amazes me that they calmly accepted this dictate from a matron. She was also by no means above criticising the visiting doctor's diagnosis and even treatment.

On one occasion whilst I was an H.S. and Matron was doing her rounds, she enquired of a patient waiting for an operation, why he was having it done. When he replied, "On the advice of his surgeon," without batting an eyelid, she told him to think carefully before making a final decision, as in her opinion he would be better off with medical treatment, and to add weight to the argument went on to say that the results of the surgeon's operations were sometimes disappointing. Matron then moved to the next bed, quite unperturbed; but not so the patient. Looking back to those years it now seems incredible that the medical staff took all this lying down, but at the time it would probably have been very difficult to do much to alter the state of affairs, as the only other with administrative powers was the Chairman and he did as the Matron wished. Competition was exceedingly keen to get on to the hospital staff and possibly the fear of being asked to resign cast a shadow over any question of a stand up confrontation. As it was, the Honorary consultant staff (at that period, all their time spent in the hospital was given free) were required to sign a book placed in the entrance hall, giving the time on entering and the time on leaving the hospital, and this had to be done on every visit. In this way an accurate check could be made on how much time each member of the staff spent in the building. Once again, it seems amazing that this was accepted, but it was, and all were meticulous in conforming to this rule. The four surgeons were all Fellows of the Royal College of Surgeons, but were also in general practice, combining GP work with hospital appointments, as was common in the smaller hospitals of that time. The possession of the F. R. C. S. does not necessarily, in itself, mean that the holder is a good surgeon, though as a cynic once remarked, it is a licence to make mistakes with a clearer conscience.

Although the Chairman, Mr. Bardell Barton, liked to look upon the patients as guests, the discipline in the wards was strict to a degree. Smoking was forbidden at all times and even card-playing was prohibited; presumably Matron was afraid it might lead to gambling, and offend her Calvinistic upbringing. There was, of course, no wireless, and the wards were bare and forbidding with an over riding smell of disinfectant. The food was anything but appetising and none too plentiful, and, like all else, was under Miss Andrew's control.

If the regime for the patients was strict and bordering on the stark, the nurses faired even worse. The hours of duty were long, the pay but a pittance (I believe for the first year not more than £10), and it was considered little short of a crime to report sick. If a probationer nurse - in those days nurses in training were known as 'Pro's' - plucked up courage to ask Matron for permission to go off sick, she was quite likely to be told that she had not been taken on to be ill, and furthermore, could not be spared from the ward which was short staffed as it was. Invariably, Miss Andrews put the pro's trouble down to constipation or to dysmenorrhea, and the poor girl would be sent off to the nurses' home to get a dose of calomel, or a couple of aspirin tablets. Smoking was strictly forbidden in the nurses' home, or anywhere else, and it was a rule that no nurse could leave the hospital grounds without wearing a hat even if out of uniform. To do so was considered by Matron to be most unladylike, and to be seen hatless in public lowered the prestige of the nursing profession and let down the high tone which she insisted her nurses maintained at all times. Whilst I was a house surgeon two nurses were dismissed, one for being found smoking in the hospital grounds even though off duty, and the other for daring to go into town without a hat though in mufti. Both were considered to be unsuitable material for continued nurse training as, seemingly, they would not accept the discipline imposed. Even though I was there at the time it seems incredible that this should happen.

The nurses' off duty was meagre in the extreme. Lectures were invariably held in off duty time (the reason for this being that they could not be spared from the ward) and worse still, if on night duty the poor girl would have to wait up till mid-day to go to a lecture, or alternatively be up by four in the afternoon. Furthermore, if a lecture happened to coincide with their day off a month, which was all the pro's were allowed, they were expected to come back, for under no circumstances could a lecture be missed. Lecture or no lecture, they had to be back anyway by 9 p.m. to attend evening prayers, taken by Matron each night at this hour in the hospital chapel. Only after three years, when the nurses were fully trained and ceased to be probationers, were they excused prayers on their day off.

Whereas the nurses were hard worked and severely disciplined, the two house surgeons were not exactly pampered. The food was of a poor quality and monotonous, and the residents' quarters far from luxuriously furnished. Apart from the usual half days, we were officially allowed one week-end in six months, and this had first to be approved by members of the house committee!

I have written at some length of the conditions prevailing over fifty years ago when I first took up a house surgeon's post, as it is in such marked contrast to those prevailing at the present time, and to the younger generation almost unbelievable. Despite all however, I was thankful to have obtained a hospital appointment, and it was satisfying to realise I was a fully-fledged doctor in actual charge of patients, though this glow of satisfaction was tempered with the realisation that although legally qualified to practice the art of medicine and surgery, I was woefully lacking in experience and only too well aware of my shortcomings. Although the other H.S. had been appointed six months prior to my arrival and was my senior, he was not a great help and I was forced to find my feet by a process of trial and error.

Initially, on being left in charge of patients without constant supervision, I found it far from easy to convey the impression that they were in safe and caring hands, well able to contend with all emergencies. I very soon discovered that a reassuring bedside manner, which is all important, does not come easily and has to be assiduously acquired, but as the weeks passed I gradually gained in confidence and began to appreciate the fears and anxieties which not infrequently beset the patients. This was especially so when their progress was marred by unforeseen complications. I tried very hard to convey my sympathy and understanding and to let it be known that I did fully appreciate just what they must be going through. Inexperienced as I was at this stage, I had already learned the importance of treating every patient as an individual. The ward sisters were of great assistance, and although not qualified like myself, their vast experience proved invaluable on many occasions, their opinions being proved to be right and the youthful doctor's wrong. I was fast learning the importance of experience, and I realised how little I, at present, possessed.

For economy reasons the house surgeons were not supplied with the customary long white coats and were expected to provide their own. To save expense I wore the short ward jackets which I had had to buy at the start of my clinical work as a student. The absence of the more conventional coat, together with my relative youth, led to an amusing incident when I was called one evening to the private wing to see an elderly patient who had fallen down and injured her hip. As soon as the ward sister drew the bedclothes aside to enable me to examine the injured leg, the patient very definitely an autocratic old lady, used to getting her own way, pulled them up again. After two further attempts had ended in similar fashion, Sister, by now a trifle irritated, firmly told the patient not to be awkward and kindly leave the bedclothes alone. She received a totally unexpected retort, when, in an aristocratic tone of voice, she was told, "I resolutely refuse to be examined by the laundry man."

As was only to be expected this episode soon got around to the nurses and was thought to be very funny. I expect I did not share this view, and probably looked upon it as being a rebuff to my bedside manner which I was trying so hard to cultivate. As I became more accustomed to the duties of a house surgeon however, I came to appreciate these lighter moments afforded a welcome relief from the daily routine, and in addition I learned by degrees to be able to laugh at myself, a most important asset for all, and especially for a hospital resident. When I first took up my duties as an H.S. I fear I considered myself superior to the senior nursing staff, for, I argued, how could it be otherwise when I was a doctor and they were but nurses. It was only a matter of days before I came to realise how wrong I was, and I quickly came to rely on their guidance together with their wealth of clinical experience.

Not so many weeks after I had been mistaken for the laundry man, I came up against another potentially difficult patient, this time a female in her late fifties admitted for a gynaecological operation. I carried out a routine pre-operative check without any trouble, but when it came to having a vaginal examination, she flatly refused, remarking that she was too old for that kind of thing, now! Once again, the ward sister came to my aid. With her experience and understanding she was able to soothe the patient with kindly explanations as to why it was necessary, and as a result of this tactful and friendly heart to heart talk, I was eventually allowed to perform a P.V. After I had finished, and wishing to reassure my patient still further, I said, in my best bedside manner, "Now that wasn't too bad really, was it?" The unexpected reply came back, "Not in the least, thank you, doctor, quite enjoyable in fact!" It was with no little difficulty that the doctor and sister managed to keep their faces straight! As I was afterwards to reflect, this was but one more instance of the value of explaining away the groundless fears which so many patients habitually harbour. As a result of tactful explanations, the dreaded internal examination had been turned into a pleasant surprise.

72

Chapter Ten

Although I had been officially appointed house surgeon, I had other duties, including the administration of anaesthetics. At that time ether was commonly used - by modern standards of anaesthesia, a relatively crude and unpleasant procedure. Despite being taught the technique as a student, I was by no means experienced and faced the first few cases with trepidation. My difficulty was the same as I had experienced when I was an anaesthetic clerk, namely, knowing how deeply under my patient was. If too little ether had been administered the patient would start making movements, much to the annoyance of the surgeon; if, on the other hand, too much, the respirations would cease, and the surgeon would have to stop what he was doing and press on the chest to get the breathing going again. This displeased the operator greatly, and in addition did nothing to increase the confidence of the anxious and sweating anaesthetist. I very soon learned the difference between giving anaesthetics, as I had done in my teaching hospital knowing that if I got into trouble I could call on expert guidance, and doing the same under completely different conditions with no-one to call upon when in difficulty - it was certainly a matter of being thrown in at the deep end. Fortunately, with practice, I managed to acquire sufficient expertise to give an adequate anaesthetic, and even more fortunately without any major disasters. Deaths whilst undergoing an operation at that time were by no means uncommon, so very different from the present day now that surgery is so safe. When this happened it cast a deep gloom over the whole of the theatre staff, and I am sure all concerned felt miserable at the sight of failure. In those days, and indeed for some years afterwards, if a patient died on the operating table, all the sterile drums were immediately taken away to be re-sterilised; the theatre was emptied of all equipment which was then washed down with a carbolic solution, and the theatre itself looked upon as contaminated. I could never understand the rationale of this pointless ritual which was carried out at all times, to the letter. I could only think it must have originated from the ancient belief that evil spirits leave the body, on death. By far the worst aspect of these unexpected disasters was the harrowing experience of having to break the news to the relatives. How I hated telling them the stark facts, and how I hated to see how shattered they were to hear the ghastly news. I felt so utterly inadequate to help at this distressing time, for what was there to say or do? Once again the nursing staff were a most welcome support.

All the surgery was performed by the visiting GP surgeons, assisted by a house surgeon. It was some months before I was allowed to operate myself. The memorable day at last arrived when I was told it was time to try my hand on the next case - a straightforward removal of an appendix. As I had been waiting for this great moment, I was naturally gratified though decidedly apprehensive and wondered how I would make out. I had never made an incision into the abdominal wall before, and although it looked simple in experienced hands I had misgivings as to how I would acquit myself. On being given the go ahead by the anaesthetist, to start, I grasped the scalpel as firmly as I could and made what I thought to be a nice clean incision over the site of the appendix. To my dismay I found I had made little more than a scratch on the surface of the skin. I had clearly not pressed hard enough with the knife when making the initial cut. I now noticed, much to my disquiet, a distinct tremor of my hand, clear evidence of nervousness, which did nothing to restore my confidence. A further attempt, with added pressure, enabled me to cut through the skin, but I found the incision was not long enough, and had to be enlarged. By now the wound had assumed a jagged appearance and was not the clean cut incision of an experienced operator. With the aid of my chief who was assisting me, I managed, with clumsy, tremulous hands to incise the structures of the abdominal wall and so to enter the peritoneal cavity - it seemed so much more difficult than I had imagined. As my scalpel cut, or perhaps more accurately all but hacked, through the muscles, I was met with copious bleeding from the severed arteries and veins. These had to be clipped with Spencer Wells forceps and then tied off with catgut. Here I was faced with two difficulties. It was no easy matter to catch the spurting vessels with the artery forceps, and having done so, equally difficult to tie them off. Working in rubber gloves, sticky with blood, made tying ligatures a tedious business, and here again I was ashamed of my lack of dexterity, even more so when, owing to inexperience, I let a fair sized artery slip from the clamp, to spurt with some force into my face covering my glasses with blood. Before I could do anything further these had to be removed, cleaned and replaced by a nurse, for I could not of course touch the spectacles with my sterile hands. At last, after my faltering steps, the abdominal cavity lay open. Now came the problem of locating the appendix and delivering it into the wound, which, for the inexperienced, is not always easy. The small intestine measures some twenty two feet, and the large another eight, and then there are all the solid organs such as the liver, the spleen and so on to be contained in a relatively small compartment, all in very close contact with each other. It is no small wonder that difficulties can arise.

My first effort to find the appendix only resulted in bringing out a loop of small bowel. This I replaced and tried again, but once again I only succeeded in delivering a different length of intestine. Noting my ineffectual attempts to find the appendix, my chief remarked with perhaps justifiable impatience, that he had better find it for me, but before he had time to do this, the patient, who was too lightly under the ether gave a violent cough, and out through the wound erupted a large amount of intestine together with the elusive appendix. After waiting for the patient to be more deeply anaesthetised, the bowel was returned and the appendix eventually removed, with nothing more serious than a few minor mishaps. If I had found it more difficult than I had anticipated to open the abdomen, I found it just as difficult, if not more so, when the time came to stitch up the wound. My inept and unpractised hands made heavy going of the work, and even when it came to the final stages of suturing the skin, the scar assumed an uneven look and showed it was the doing of an amateur. My final efforts to make the incision a little more presentable were abruptly terminated by the theatre sister remarking, "Come along now, that will do a treat and all!" She was a worthy person who had been at the hospital for years, combining the onerous post of theatre sister with the out-patient and casualty departments. She possessed boundless energy, and when faced with something which was not quite the thing, settled the matter to her own satisfaction by remarking 'that will do a treat and all'.

At the conclusion of my first ever operation I was drenched with perspiration, and far from pleased with the manner in which I had conducted the appendectomy. I realised that I had a long way to go before I mastered an adequate surgical technique, but despite these doubts I looked forward to further advances into operative surgery, and was quite determined to do better next time. I, needless to say, in the succeeding days, took more interest in this patient than in the others, for it was my personal case, and I watched his progress with anxious eyes. Apart from perhaps rather more post-operative discomfort, all went well. I hoped none of the nurses would let on that an H.S. had performed the operation, for patients, naturally enough, liked to think that they had been operated upon by a visiting surgeon and not a young doctor starting his surgical training.

Following this red letter day in the theatre I was given the opportunity of doing further operations, always under supervision, and by degrees I gained more confidence in my abilities as a surgeon. Long hours were spent, both in the day and the night, bent over the operating table assisting at all kinds of operations - at times attempting against hopeless odds to save a patient already doomed. There were times, junior as I undoubtedly was, when I considered the surgeon was attempting the impossible and it would have perhaps been wiser not to have operated at all, but I could, of course, do nothing to alter his decision, though I sometimes wished I could. I was to recall the teaching I had received, that the first duty of a surgeon - if you can't do good, don't do harm. There was one particular surgeon who would have been wise to bear this apt aphorism in mind, for he would 'have a go', as he put it, on the principle that to do something was better than to do nothing, though masterly inactivity might well have been in the best interests of the patient.

I shall never forget the occasion when I was to give an anaesthetic for this surgeon to perform a major operative procedure which I considered, under the circumstances, was, to say the least, unwise. He was never punctual, and on this particular day, was already half an hour late. I was inexperienced and very tactless at the time, and I should, of course, never have spoken as I did to the nursing staff about one of their Honoraries, as specialists were then called. But I was worried at the thought of giving the anaesthetic, as it could well end by having a death on the table. In addition, the patient was becoming more nervous as the surgeon failed to arrive; for my part I was none too happy as to how I would manage the anaesthetic. As time wore on and still no signs of the surgeon, in a mood of exasperation I all but exploded remarking, "Mr. Stanmore (for that was the surgeon's name) is a most inconsiderate man. It's appalling bad manners to be so late without sending his apologies. But, of course, that's typical of Mr. Stanmore, and as for doing, or perhaps more aptly, attempting to do this very complicated operation, he really shouldn't be doing it. He is certainly no great surgeon, and I would definitely not want him to operate on me, not even for a simple appendectomy." I was under the impression I was addressing the theatre Sister, who I thought was standing behind me. Imagine my consternation when, getting no reply to this grossly unprofessional and quite unforgivable outburst, I turned round and saw to my horror not the sister, but Mr. Stanmore himself. He had come quietly into the theatre unseen and must have heard all my critical remarks. The theatre sister had been powerless to stop me making such a fool of myself. It says much for Mr. Stanmore that I was not sacked on the spot - I could really say nothing to excuse myself. Sister was obviously very embarrassed. Mr. Stanmore however, greatly to his credit, pretended he had not heard my judgement on him as a man and a surgeon, and proceeded to get ready to operate as if nothing untoward had occurred - perhaps he made allowances for my youth and lack of social graces. Whatever his reasons, he came out of this debacle with great credit. Furthermore, he never once mentioned it on future occasions, nor did he appear to bear any malice towards me. Understandably, I felt distressed and ashamed and was exceedingly uncomfortable having to sit at the head of the patient giving the anaesthetic throughout a prolonged operation; so far as I can remember, and the incident remains only too clearly in my mind, few words were spoken. Fortunately the operation went without any serious mishaps, and my fears of a death were unfounded.

At that time I had not learned to control my feelings, and too frequently said things in the heat of the moment, which would have been far better left unspoken. I had yet to learn the wise old saying: 'I have often regretted my speech, but never my silence'. I would have done well, in addition, to observe the golden rule, 'act not in furious passion, it's putting to sea in a storm'. But I was only slowly to grow in wisdom.

Looking back down the years I cannot but be amazed at the thought of how naive I was, how unworldly wise, and, I suppose, socially immature. Throughout the time of my first hospital appointment I did not take any special interest in the nurses, and certainly never asked any one of them out with me. I suppose the psychologists would say that not having had sex explained to me, or even mentioned, as a child, and being brought up to the idea that it was a dirty word and not to be talked about, I grew to be afraid of getting involved in any active participation. The dread of putting a girl in the family way, or of catching VD was uppermost in my thoughts.

My only sexual outlets during this period rested on D.I.Y. procedures. Even this harmless practice, as it is now considered to be in these enlightened days, caused me not a little anxiety. But a healthy young man must have a sexual outlet, and if for various reasons he fears going with a woman, which is the natural source of gratification, his sexual drive is bound to surface in other ways. There was never any question in the process of growing up of discussing such intimate subjects with my parents; it would have been completely unheard of and would never have been brought up. Unfortunately I only really came to know my Father just a few years before he died. Previously we did not understand each other, and I looked upon him as a person who earned the money to pay my medical fees, and someone who must not be upset for he had a quick temper. I suppose, earlier on in my life, I was rather afraid or possibly rather in awe of him. This I greatly regret for I came too late to appreciate his fine character. As I have mentioned earlier on, my parents unhappily had absolutely nothing in common and arguments and rows were all too frequent.

For her part, Matron saw to it that her nurses were well protected, as far as it was humanly possible, from any petting sessions, and there was never any question of illicit cups of tea, and a 'quiet chat' in the ward kitchens. The uniforms, also, did absolutely nothing for the figure, long ill fitting dresses made of a hard cheap material, and long aprons most effectively covering up the shapely curves of the body. What little could be seen of the legs were encased in thick woollen stockings. The only occasions on which I had anything but truly professional relationship with any member of the nursing staff was the odd time when I held a skein of knitting wool between my hands, as the night sister expertly rolled it into a neat ball, and that was as far as it went! Looking back, what a waste of potentially exciting opportunities; but then I looked at things in a different light, and discipline in the hospital was exceedingly strict. I suppose I had yet to learn the secret of living life to the full.

Chapter Eleven

As Christmas drew near I looked forward to my first in hospital as a house surgeon. Some weeks previously the patients had been given crepe paper and had been busy making chains, the more expert making paper flowers. As the day drew near, the strict, almost prison like, atmosphere, became less oppressive, and the wards began to empty, all those well enough going home in time for Christmas. Those who remained, if fit to be out of bed, helped the nurses to put up the decorations. On the actual day, following the official visit of Father Christmas and then the Mayor's party, the patients were served with the traditional fare, and on this very special occasion the men were each given a bottle of beer, an unheard of concession at normal times.

As a houseman I was expected to participate in the ward festivities, which I managed to do, helped by a dose or two of Christmas spirit. The nursing staff had their Dinner on Boxing Day, followed by the usual dance held in the nurses' home. At the dinner, Miss Andrews, the Matron, was as ever, in full command, and resplendent in uniform, presided over the assembled company in a manner reminiscent of a head mistress. Needless to say, she was the only one not in mufti. When the time came to serve the Christmas pudding, with the traditional 3d and 6d bits for the lucky ones, she had her own way of seeing that the money went to her favourites. The coins were not put in the actual pudding, but placed on a nearby saucer; the Home Sister, who was helping Matron by holding the plates, would say to Miss Andrews, "This is for Nurse so-and-so," and if she was in favour, from the saucer would be taken a 3d or 6d piece, depending on where she was in the Matron's hierarchy. Having placed the coin on a portion of pudding, a further helping was placed on top making the picture authentic. As the serving was done out of sight of the nurses, behind a red screen borrowed from one of the wards, this procedure went undetected except for a few in the know. Needless to say, the majority of the nurses got nothing. At that time, when they were paid a veritable pittance, sixpence was well worth having, for in those days sixpence bought quite a lot.

The dance followed the dinner and was looked forward to with joyful enthusiasm. Again, Miss Andrews sat throughout in her starched uniform, keeping an ever watchful eye on her nurses, and making perfectly sure that their behaviour was befitting a member of the nursing profession; it was her custom to vet the evening dresses to make certain they were not in any way revealing. Unhappily, this proved to be the case with one poor nurse. She was an attractive girl, and although by present day standards her evening dress would have been considered most conservative, revealing next to nothing, Matron thought otherwise, and her eyes followed the doomed pro' round and round the dance floor, until finally she could stand it no more and beckoned the poor girl to come off the floor. She was then told that her dress was most unseemly and was letting down the tone of the profession and she could not continue to wear it.

She must therefore go immediately to her room, take it off, and not return to the dance until she was properly attired. As the wretched nurse had but one evening gown it meant she had had the dance, and I am sure must have felt very miserable for the rest of the night. I have since wondered how Miss Andrews would have reacted to the present day fashions of the low cut cleavage, where the mammary glands can be viewed coming up for air. It was such a dress which caused a small boy to ask, "Mummy, why is that lady showing us her bottles?"

During my student days I had drunk next to nothing, so I had no real appreciation of the affects of alcohol, being totally unused to intoxicating liquors. At Christmas, however, I felt I should not stand aside during the festivities, and I began to explore what had, up till now, been all but unknown territories. I had yet to learn, to my cost, the penalty of mixing drinks indiscriminately, and that gin and whisky were certainly not on meeting terms. I was only too soon to experience a fearful hangover following a night of reckless drinking. This was but one example of my ignorance of the facts of life, for I should have had the good sense to take alcohol in a reasonable and moderate way, and not to plunge right in at the deep end. On the evening of the dance I had had a fairly heavy intake, mixing my drinks with no thought for tomorrow. I was anxious to be well oiled for the occasion, for I was by no means an accomplished performer and looked on alcohol as a valid help.

I certainly felt in the best of spirits when, dressed in tails, I entered the recreation room. After I had had time to get acclimatised as it were, I felt I must ask Miss Andrews to dance, as she was technically my hostess for the evening. I accordingly made my way, a little uncertainly, as the drinks I had consumed were now beginning to take effect, to where she was sitting, intent as ever on watching her nurses' behaviour. I had no difficulty in locating Miss Andrews, even though my eyes could have focused a little more efficiently, for Matron was the only person present in the room in uniform. With my feet apart for a more certain stance, I made the customary bow, and requested the pleasure of a dance. Now it seemed Matron never danced; either she couldn't or, more likely, thought she shouldn't mix with the nurses. So, as was her habitual custom, she refused. But I was in no mood to take no for an answer. I had been taught always to be sure to dance with my hostess whether I wished or not, and although I definitely did not want to, I was determined to do the correct thing and to show that I knew what was what; and besides, it seemed a shame not to take advantage of all that booze. Miss Andrews must, at this stage, have realised I had no intention of accepting her refusals, and thinking it would be the lesser of two evils to humour me, reluctantly rose from her seat and together we made for the dance floor. Unfortunately, our upright posture was to be short lived. I had taken but a few stumbling steps before my sense of balance appeared to have gone awry, and the next I knew we had both fallen and lay in a tangled mass on the floor, much to the amusement of the nurses, for they never for one moment imagined they would see the always so correct Miss Andrews lying in an unseemly posture an her back, her uniform in disarray. I am quite sure they would have loved to have shown their appreciation and approval by a burst of applause but this was, of course, unthinkable! My stock undoubtedly fell to an all time low as far as Matron was concerned, but on the other hand the nursing staff thought it was great, almost too good to be true, and it certainly boosted my popularity.

I have but a hazy recollection of the rest of that evening, but still a vivid memory of the following morning. Not only had I attacks of severe nausea and vomiting to contend with, but in addition a terrible headache; it felt as though I had a number of little men inside my skull trying to hammer their way out, but with no success. If this is the result of an unwise and too heavy consumption of alcohol, never again I told myself. I felt exceedingly fragile and wondered how on earth I was going to last out an operating session which faced me in a few hours time. Breakfast was quite out of the question, the mere thought brought on waves of nausea. Even shaving had been a most unpleasant ordeal - I had been forced, half way through, to abandon the razor and seek refuge in a chair until the bouts of nausea had lessened. I was also conscious of looking ghastly, and the terrible throbs from my head continued relentlessly on. All in all I was more than sorry for myself and cursed my crass stupidity of the preceding evening. I was also in doubt as to how Miss Andrews would greet me after the humiliation she had suffered at my hands, for I felt certain she would consider it as such.

Somehow I managed to get through the day, but it was a long time before I could bring myself to touch alcohol again. Miss Andrews very wisely never mentioned my bad behaviour towards her, though she probably looked upon me now as one to be watched in the future, thinking 'if he could do that to the Matron, what indeed could he do to her nurses!' But she need not have troubled herself on that score.

Deaths at any time in hospitals are very distressing both for the staff and the patients, for those who are very ill cannot do otherwise but wonder if they will be the next to go. There were no side rooms into which the dying could be moved, so the whole ward was only too aware of what was happening to the patient in the end bed surrounded by screens. Deaths occurring at Christmas time are all the more distressing, if this is possible, for they take place amidst a background of streamers and decorations and a general air of gaiety, generated by the festive season. One case has especially stuck in my mind after so many years. John, an only son in his early teens, was brought in by ambulance, having been knocked down whilst crossing the road. I subsequently learned that he had been given some extra pocket money, and was rushing to the local shop to buy a present for his mother, and in the excitement of the moment forgot to look to see if it was safe to cross. On admission, he was deeply unconscious, with laboured breathing, so typical of a severe head injury; his face was covered with blood and dirt, and he was bleeding from the nose and ears. All too clearly the signs of a fractured skull with, almost certainly, severe damage to the brain.

John was taken to the ward, bright with balloons together with all the other adornments of Christmas decorations, and nursed behind screens. There was, unhappily, little that could be done, and the outlook was well nigh hopeless. John's distracted parents, beside themselves with grief, sat by the screened bed, and to their pitiful pleas, "You won't let our son die, will you? He's all we've got, he will get better won't he?" it was heart breaking to be forced to reply that it was touch and go, and unless there were some signs of slight improvement shortly, the chances were very slim indeed. How I hated having to say these words. His Mother alternately held her son's hand and stroked his forehead, pushing away a strand of hair which had fallen over his eyes. The Father sat quite still, clutching his hat in both hands; he had the appearance of a man utterly devastated. John continued to go deeper and ever deeper into coma, his breathing now became stertorous and was audible some distance from the screens. It was only a matter of time before he would die from a severe brain injury.

His parents continued to sit by their beloved son's death bed, only occasionally being persuaded to leave the ward for a cup of tea and a short break from their terrible ordeal. During one of their rare absences, Matron put her head round the screens to see what was going on. When she saw how hopeless the position was, with both arms folded across her ample bosom, her sole contribution to this heart rending was the remark, "Youth dies hard, yes, indeed, youth dies hard." She then withdrew and continued on her round. Slowly but remorselessly John's life drew to its untimely end, and he died in the early hours of Christmas Day. To the very end his distraught parents continued to hope for a miracle. I felt deeply for them in their grievous loss, made, if possible, even more poignant by the Christmas decorations which adorned the backcloth to John's dying moments. From now on, when each Christmas came round, it would no longer be the joyous occasion of former times, but a painful reminder of the tragic loss of their only son, and the customary decorations an added hurt, for they would be for ever associated with the painful memory of sitting behind screens waiting for the end to come, that terrible time never to be forgotten.

As the weeks went by and I gained increasing experience, I believe I also gained in compassion for the bereaved relatives, and I came to dread seeing the red screens permanently left round a bed, for this inevitably indicated that a patient was dangerously ill and probably going to die. The whole ward was subdued, all eyes watching the occupant of the end bed, strategically placed so that the body could be taken to the mortuary as inconspicuously as possible. Side rooms would have been so very much better, but were not available. Later, when I had moved to another hospital, dangerously ill and dying patients were always moved to a side room in order to avoid disturbing the rest of the patients. But even this was not without its drawbacks, for it came to be known as the 'death ward', and all ill patients would say, "I hope you are not thinking of moving me into the death ward, because if you do, I shan't come out except in a box, once I get in there."

At this period, long before the days of antibiotics, intravenous infusions, gastric suction, and modern anaesthetic techniques, the surgical mortality was not inconsiderable, and a perforated appendix with peritonitis carried a high death rate. This was largely due to the lack of the present day antibiotic drugs, but also to a misconception of the correct understanding and management of the problem, and in consequence adopting the wrong approach. One of the commonest complications following an operation for acute appendicitis, more especially if complicated by peritonitis resulting from a burst appendix, is distension of the bowel, the so-called paralytic ileus. The 30 feet or so of small and large intestine are coiled closely together so they can be contained in a relatively small area known as the abdominal cavity. The contents of the bowel are propelled onwards by rhythmic contractions throughout its length to the termination of the intestinal tract at the rectum - not a very dissimilar process from that of a conveyor belt in an automated factory. In the presence however, of adverse factors, most often bacterial infection progressing to general peritonitis, these peristaltic contractions, or bowel movements, cease, and in consequence the intestines become distended, no flatus or motion being passed. If not treated promptly with adequate intravenous fluids, gastric aspiration, and the all important antibiotics, together with sedatives to rest the bowel, the condition inevitably progresses and ultimately may prove fatal.

The one thing not to do is to try to get the paralysed bowel to start to work again by administering strong purgatives, enemas and other stimulants. Owing to the infection the bowel can no longer contract, and must be rested and given time to recover. On no account must it be exposed to vain attempts to get it moving again, somewhat akin to the unrewarding whipping of a tired horse.

However, in the '20's and early part of the '30's when I was an H.

S., these vital facts were not appreciated, and it was argued that if a patient was ill with a distended abdomen, clearly the thing to do was to relieve the distension by stimulating the intestines to start working again, the patient should then begin to improve. Accordingly, no effort was spared to achieve this end. The ill and frequently vomiting patients were subjected to a series of enemas, starting with the simple enema saponis, and getting no result, inflicting on the, by now, rapidly deteriorating patient, the more drastic turpentine enema, this being a soap enema with the addition of a teaspoonful of turpentine, resulting in a very irritating fluid solution - now so rightly relegated to the past ages. Despite these misguided efforts, no benefit accrued, and the distension and vomiting continued unabated on their relentless course. Apart from worsening the condition, the only positive result of ordering a turpentine enema was that the turpentine could be smelled throughout the ward, not being confined inside the screens round the bed. At this stage, the time had usually arrived when, in anticipation of a fatal outcome, the screens were no longer removed. In the terminal stages, the close relatives were given chairs to sit by the dying patient, hoping against all odds that death could be defeated. When the end came, how I hated to witness the distress as they were led away, so often in a collapsed state, on the helping arm of a young but kindly nurse. It was always such a sad occasion, and a sign of dismal failure, for as doctors and nurses we had not succeeded in saving a life, and if this life had been in its prime, the tragedy seemed all the greater. By no means all the cases of abdominal distension died - those who did usually had advanced general peritonitis. Happily, the less severe cases, as a rule, got better, though their recovery was often protracted, and there was even the odd occasion when a simple enema was given to reduce distension and yielded dividends. I remember an instance of this, when, as a final year student, I was accompanying the H.S. on his evening round. Whilst he was discussing the order of the next morning's operating list with the staff nurse, she at intervals interrupted the conversation to make a note on a chart lying on the desk; the H.S. demanded to know what she was doing, as he did not appear to have her full attention. The nurse replied that a patient with abdominal distension had just been given an enema and she was making a note of the number of times he was passing flatus.

After an abdominal operation there is usually a degree of

distension brought about by the handling of the intestines, but this is not in the same category as the distension arising from peritonitis, and is quick to subside. The more gently the operation is performed, the less post-operative discomfort is experienced, and I was taught early on in my surgical training always to 'caress the tissues'. The average quantity of gas produced in the intestinal tract varies from half to one litre a day, and when normal peristaltic contractions are temporarily interrupted, this gas accumulates, producing discomfort and even pain, which is greatly relieved when flatus is passed, and is a very great comfort to the patient, and is often an important diagnostic aid to the surgeon.

Some patients, especially the elder ones, were, in the past, more embarrassed than they are today when asked about such personal matters, though it was often important to know if they had passed wind, or what the more down to earth called 'blown off'. If they appeared to be diffident when asked if they had passed any wind, to put them more at ease I would recount the tale of the somewhat deaf old lady buying six yards of calico, and as the shop assistant turned round to wrap it up, she passed wind. Immediately the old lady said, "No dear, don't split it, I will take it in the one piece." After this, I had only to enquire if they had split any calico today when doing my rounds. To the shy individual this proved to be an easier way, and was as a rule accepted in a light hearted manner. Indeed, a grand old man greeted me one morning by remarking that he was feeling on top of the world since he had split his bottom sheet in shreds! When fit and well we take our bodily functions for granted, and we do not talk about our bowel habits. It is a different story however, when recovering from major abdominal surgery - the passing of flatus or even the first bowel movement may well be a red letter day.

Normally the last six to eight inches in the large intestine, called the rectum as its course is straight, should remain empty of contents until just before the bowels are ready to act; it is the entry of faecal contents into the rectum which provides the sensation that it is time to go to the toilet. This physiological process appeared to be well appreciated by one of the patients, a builder by trade, for when I asked if his bowels had moved he replied, "Not as yet, but it won't be long now as I have just got the invoice through."

86

Chapter Twelve

The Honoraries, or visiting specialists, received no remuneration for their services to the hospital. They made however, a good income from operating in private nursing homes, and from general practice. They were conscientious in carrying out their hospital commitments and spent long hours in the wards and theatres, leading a busy life and being frequently pushed for time.

The Senior Surgeon was very keen on the money. He had a large private practice and his own nursing home, and periodically could not resist telling me how well he was doing. On returning from a holiday in the South, he proudly told me that in the four days he had been back at work he had more than paid for his holiday with still more to come. As I escorted him to his chauffeur driven Sunbeam car, I resolved that should I ever reach his exalted position, I would not discuss how much money I was making with my house surgeon who was earning a relative pittance, and was forced to watch every penny.

Sunday mornings, being free from GP surgeries, was the usual day for full ward rounds, and I was expected to be in attendance every week without fail. I was reminded of this some years later when, at another hospital, the senior surgeon, an elderly bachelor, also did a ward round every Sunday. Although his H.S. was officially off duty every other weekend, he was, nevertheless, expected to accompany his chief on every occasion. At last he felt he really must make a stand as it was getting beyond a joke. So when his chief said he would see him on the ward round as usual at 9 o'clock on Sunday plucking up his courage the H.S. managed to say, "I am very sorry Sir, I am off duty and have arranged to play a round of golf in the morning!"

"Very well, then," came the reply, "I will see you at half past ten!"

In those days when I was a house surgeon, there were no curtains to draw round each bed; the only means of privacy provided were heavy wooden screens kept at the end of the ward. When a patient was being examined by a GP specialist it was one of my duties to help the nurse to carry these screens to and from the bed. They were solid structures and were heavy for the nurses who constantly had to carry them around. It was long before the days of light aluminium screens on wheels, which in turn were replaced by bedside curtains. Usually the Sunday morning rounds passed without any special incidents and I can recall nothing of note, except on one occasion when I asked a somewhat pompous Honorary if he would examine a patient as I was uncertain as to the diagnosis. Having lugged the screens from the end of the long ward, I placed them around the bed, and the self important chief, beautifully attired in his best Sunday suit, approached the patient saying, "Well, my man, what's the matter? What do you complain of?"

"It's the wind, Doctor, I am always bringing up a wonderful amount of wind." As the doctor bent down to examine the abdomen, the patient exploded a tremendous belch, right into the face of the Honorary. Drawing himself to his full height, he remarked with feeling, "You could at least have spared me the demonstration." I had to beat a hasty retreat from the screens as I had the greatest difficulty in keeping a straight face. The chief however, was far from amused and was exceedingly uncomplimentary about the patient's manners.

It was this Honorary who, faced with the unusual problem of unexplained and gross swellings of the legs occurring in a young girl, and having recently read that the condition sometimes responded to pineapple juice in liberal amounts, ordered a cupful to be taken twice a day. The sister and I wondered how this was to be obtained but Matron, as ever in overall charge, found little difficulty for she simply ordered tin upon tin of pineapple chunks. The juice was given to the patient and the desiccated chunks to the staff. By the time they reached us they were as dry and as hard as lumps of wood, and I became disenchanted, as the days passed, with these dehydrated lumps of tinned pineapple. They seemed never ending. After a while I managed to persuade the Honorary to discontinue the treatment as it did not appear to be doing the patient any good, and most definitely not the staff. It was to be many a year before I could bring myself to eat another pineapple chunk.

House appointments were for a period of six months and I was now coming to the closing weeks. Perhaps unwisely, I decided to move up to the Senior House Officer's post and to stay on for a further six months. I was gaining confidence in myself with ever increasing clinical experience, and was happy enough in the hospital despite the many drawbacks. Moreover, I suspect subconsciously, I did not wish to leave my familiar surroundings and to have to start to break new ground; I had not yet been long enough to get into a rut. Years later I was told that the toughest form of mountain climbing is getting out of a rut, which struck me as being very appropriate.

I was now in a position of rather more authority and responsibility, and was becoming reasonably proficient in administering anaesthetics; and on the occasions when I was given simple straightforward operations to do I was by no means so ham-fisted. My social life remained very mundane. I continued to have little or no interest in the nursing staff, and apart from the Christmas dance there were no social functions in the hospital. My off-duty hours were spent mostly at home. My Father, although retired, continued to live in the nearby village, and was naturally interested in my activities as a house surgeon, and was very pleased when my chief invited both of us to go as his guests to the annual Medical Dinner, held in the leading hotel in the town. It is curious how certain things remain in the memory for a seemingly indefinite time, while others are lost for ever. In this instance I can remember absolutely nothing of that dinner except for a story told by a guest speaker which, in the presence of mixed company, I considered to be in very poor taste. Perhaps in those days, when one's behaviour was expected to be far more correct than the present time, I was bordering on the prude. The story in question was about an election meeting in support of that well known Labour candidate of his day J. H. Thomas. At the end of an impassioned address the speaker concluded, "I ask you, Ladies and Gentlemen, who has done more for the role of the working class population than J. H. Thomas?" A voice from the back of the hall was heard to shout out, "John Thomas!" I have no idea, since I must have heard literally hundreds of stories, some certainly much nearer the bone, why this particular one has such a firm place in my memory. Possibly because it was the first time I had heard a risky story told before a mixed audience.

The second six months of my appointment appeared to pass so much faster than the first six months. This is, of course, always the case, from life itself onwards - the first half progresses but slowly, while on the other hand, the second half gathers increasing momentum.

I had now to make a definite decision as to my next move.

Although the original intention had been to join my Father with a view to taking over the practice, I had known for some time that this was not possible due to his enforced retirement from ill health. I felt at this early stage in my career that I would like to continue to gain further experience in hospital jobs before making a final decision as to my future. I wanted more and more to be a good sound doctor, and what better way than to continue in hospital at least for another six months, and possibly even longer. But the vital question was - where? Appointments at good hospitals were not easy to get, the competition was keen. My first application was to a well-known, though not a teaching hospital, in London. To my surprise, in due course, I received a letter requesting me to call on five, or it may have been six, Harley Street and Wimpole Street specialists, to introduce myself prior to the interview, when an appointment would be made from a short list of candidates. This was the accepted custom of the time, presumably to provide an additional opportunity of assessing the applicants' true worth on a man to man basis. As I was living fifty miles from London, and did not want to make separate journeys up to town for each appointment, I contrived, with considerable difficulty, to fix them all for the same day, though inevitably there were long intervals in between each one. More than once, when I arrived at the stated time, the specialist had been called to an urgent case, or was not available for some reason or another, and I had to come back later. I still have a vivid memory of that day, spending long hours trudging up and down Harley Street trying to fill in the intervals between the appointments, and how slowly this time passed. I was worried, too, that all the walking and hanging around would have an adverse effect on the smart and tidy appearance I was so anxious to present. At an appointed hour, I climbed the steps to an impressive door, and nervously rang the bell, which was opened by an awe-inspiring butler who, enquiring as to my business, somewhat condescendingly conducted me to an enormous room, or so it seemed in my agitated state. The eminent specialist sat at the far end, half hidden by a large desk, and as I walked towards him I felt I was walking almost the length of a cricket pitch for I knew I was being closely observed as I did so, and this made me even more self-conscious. It was a relief to reach the desk, and after a hand shake, to be asked to sit down on a chair, facing the great man. I am unable to recall one word of these interviews but I do remember that it was only a short while before the butler was summoned to show me to the door. All the visits I made on that day conformed to similar patterns, the chief difference being in the size of the consulting rooms, all of which were large and richly carpeted. The interview proper was held at the hospital about a week later, at eight o'clock in the evening. When it came to my turn to be called into the board room, I was asked what school I had been to, what games I had played and in what position, and had I been in any school teams. I was also asked what hobbies I had and what forms of relaxation I took when off duty. Not a word about my past experience as a house officer for the last year. Needless to say I did not get the job! They were obviously looking for a well balanced and mature doctor.

How very different this experience was from the present. Gone long ago are the days when would-be applicants were asked to call on Harley Street consultants, and gone too are the butlers to open the front doors. These old customs have been taken over by computerised forms.

I was, of course, disappointed at not getting the appointment, but by no means surprised. A week or two after my unsuccessful exploits in town, I saw an advertisement in the British Medical Journal for a house surgeon in a well known hospital in the provinces, and on this occasion was fortunate indeed to be given a personal recommendation. This particular hospital must have been unique as the Honorary Consultant staff did not hold interviews in the accepted manner, preferring to appoint their house officers on recommendations from reliable sources. They reasoned that it was difficult, if not next to impossible, to assess a candidate's abilities and personality from a short interview, and the one who interviews well may not necessarily turn out to be the right one in the long run. I was delighted to receive a telegram offering me the post of H.S. and I promptly replied, on the prepaid wire, my acceptance. The contrast between these two applications could not have been greater.

When the time finally came for me to say farewell to the hospital which had been the scene of my first year's activities as a doctor, I did so with few regrets, though I was grateful for the experience I had gained. On the whole, I had spent a reasonably happy time learning how to treat my patients with compassion, and to deal with certain members of staff with forbearance. As to my creature comforts, I have never since lived in such spartan surroundings, and certainly never had such poor food; it really was an all time low. In those times, of course, the voluntary hospitals were compelled to consider every penny spent, and in this particular hospital the Matron and Chairman working together had developed this into a fine art, far too fine in actual fact. I now looked forward to my forthcoming appointment in a larger hospital with pleasurable anticipation.

Chapter Thirteen

On taking up my new appointment I found it very different from the one I had so recently vacated. The resident medical staff was considerably larger, and the general atmosphere was much more congenial. The patients were faced with far fewer restrictions, there was no ban on playing cards or similar games, and smoking was permitted within certain hours. Overall it appeared to be a happy and well organised hospital.

Although the Matron was in full charge of the very excellent nursing staff, she exercised nothing like the power and authority of my former Matron. The food was certainly first class, and, as far as the residents were concerned, got even better as time went by. Fortunately for the rest of us, the house-keeping sister who looked after the catering, had a crush on one of the house physicians, and periodically we would ask him to call on this sister to congratulate her on a splendid meal, and to convey the compliments of the mess. These visits were well rewarded - they were worth their weight in food!

I was house surgeon to two chiefs. In this large hospital they were entirely committed to specialising in surgery, there being no question of combining surgery with general practice.

Although I had been appointed by these surgeons, I had not so much as set eyes on my future chiefs, nor had they on me, before arriving at the hospital, and I naturally wondered what they would be like, and what they would think of their new house surgeon whom they had appointed via the Post Office. I was soon to discover that they were completely different in temperament. The senior of the two, Mr. Wansfell, although a strict disciplinarian and expecting at all times a very high standard of patient care, was a delightful chief to work for. He was placid, considerate, and above all conscientious to a degree: his first thoughts were always how his patients could best be treated.

I still recall my time as Mr. Wansfell's H.S. with the deepest pleasure, and I have not forgotten his aphorism that 'relative poverty is worth £500 a year to the young'. He considered that a too easy affluent life when young was bad for the character. To succeed it was necessary to work hard, and there was a risk in apparent success coming too soon and too easily. Needless to say, £500 a year at that time was a great deal of money.

My other chief, Mr. Brooke Hill, was a totally different proposition, being erratic to a degree. He could be, and often was, perfectly charming, but if something displeased him, as was often the case, he would fly into a temper and become most unreasonable, not to say inconsiderate, to an extent I had seldom seen before. Above all, and the most unforgivable, he could at times be anything but kind to his patients. Mr. Hill - he was seldom called Mr. Brooke Hill - either got on well with his house surgeon, or disliked him intensely. There were never any half measures, he was not that kind of man. Most unfairly he formed his opinion within a very few days of his H. S. taking up the post. If the unfortunate man happened to make even quite a minor error that was that, and from then on he was damned and could do no right. Shortly after taking up my appointment I learned of the occasion when, for no apparent reason, Mr. Hill took a violent dislike to his house surgeon. When the six months appointment was coming to an end, as was the custom, the house surgeon asked if he could have a testimonial. Hill is said to have replied, "I will certainly give you one with pleasure, but if I do you will most certainly never get another job. Your wisest course is to ask me not to give you one."

I was fortunate in as much as Mr. Hill approved of me right from the start, and we got on well together, but why this should have been I do not know. Some months later he confessed that he made up his mind if he was going to like his H.S. or not on the first meeting, and once made up it was never changed.

I was thrown in at the deep end as on my first day on duty I found I was due to assist Mr. Hill with his morning's operating list. He was a very fast surgeon, impatient of the slightest delay, and expected everything and everybody to be correct in every detail, and woe betide them if they weren't. Being my first morning in Mr. Hill's theatre, I had no means of knowing what was his normal behaviour, though I certainly sensed he was in a bad mood, for nothing met with his approval. To begin with he was not satisfied with the way the patient had been positioned on the table; the sand bags had not been properly placed to steady the head for a thyroid operation, he pointed out impatiently. When a nurse attempted to correct this, Mr. Hill, getting ever redder in the face, told her she was making it worse, any fool could do better, he wasn't asking for much, only just a little intelligence, which he wasn't getting. This only served to make the Nurse's efforts all the more ineffectual, for by now she was getting into an agitated state - not without good cause. Despite being all ready to operate, gowned and gloved, in a final fit of temper Mr. Hill announced that as he was unlucky enough to be surrounded by a set of incompetent idiots, he would have to position the patient himself, and proceeded to snatch a sand bag from the nurse's hands, and to arrange the position to his liking, but not before two or three had been thrown onto the floor for one reason or another. He then had to scrub up again and regown. I was, by this time, wondering what I had let myself in for. I had started to assist Mr. Hill, with not a little trepidation, for I did not know what was to happen next. The operation had not been in progress long when Mr. Hill requested the table to be tilted. By mistake a nurse turned the table the wrong way, an easy and not very serious error. She was met with, "That's splendid, nurse, just carry on, that's what kills the patient!" Despite all his bad tempered outbursts Mr. Hill was an able surgeon and the difficult operation was successfully concluded. I think some, at least, of his unreasonable outbursts were due to pent up tension at the prospect of performing difficult and often hazardous procedures.

I was soon to discover that it was by no means unusual for the theatre sister to be in tears at the end of a long operating session when Mr. Hill had been 'blowing his top'. Surprisingly, he was not all that unpopular, though certainly to be feared at times; but despite all this he could on occasions be charm itself. After my first morning I became used to his outbursts of temper, though I never knew what was likely to happen from one moment to the next. All in such a contrast to my other chief, Mr. Wansfell, who rarely if ever lost his temper and always treated the staff with consideration - he was indeed a true gentleman.

Shortly after I became his H.S. Mr. Hill arrived for one of his operating sessions accompanied by a visiting surgeon who had come to watch the morning's operations. Mr. Hill was always dead on time, and expected everybody to be ready and waiting for him. Unfortunately, on this particular day the theatre was not immediately available, due to an emergency case which had taken longer than was anticipated. Sister apologised for the unavoidable delay and explained that it would only be about half an hour before the list could start. Mr. Hill however, was furious that the theatre was not available and demanded to know why he had not been informed of the delay; he was most certainly not going to hang about wasting his valuable time. He went on to say that as it was perfectly clear it was not convenient for the staff to start his list as usual at 9 a.m., he would be the very last person to inflict himself on Sister and her staff if he was not wanted at this time, as was apparently the case, he would therefore come back and start his list at 9 p.m. provided, of course, Sister would have the theatre ready by then. With a 'good morning' he turned on his heels and left. I wondered what the visiting surgeon made of this most unreasonable behaviour. At that time there was no night theatre staff, and the operations, which did indeed begin at nine o'clock in the evening, continued into the small hours of the morning. I was left to finish the last two relatively minor cases. It is now so long ago that it is not possible to remember any details of this unhappy episode, but I imagine the nurses would have to be on duty in the morning as usual despite having been up half the night. The theatre sister certainly would, not to mention the tired house surgeon!

As I have said, Mr. Hill was a good and rapid operator but subject to outbursts of temper which at the time he seemed unable to control, though I believe he was sorry after these explosions when he had had time to calm down. He did quite a number of operations using local anaesthetics, general anaesthesia, at that time, was not anything approaching the high standard of the present day. If the conscious patient unduly complained of feeling pain and showed signs of becoming restless on the operating table, Mr. Hill was anything but sympathetic, made no attempt at reassurance, and just carried on. The nurse sitting at the head of the patient was left to do the best she could. I shall never forget the day when a well built man, a sailor home on leave, was being operated upon by Mr. Hill for an obstructed abdominal hernia under a local anaesthetic.

The operation was proving to be more difficult than had been anticipated, and the patient was not being very co-operative, which was doing nothing to improve the surgeon's temper. I felt that at any moment there could well be an outburst. I was correct, for when the time came to sew up the incision the patient could not, or would not, relax and keep still, making it next to impossible to suture the wound.

The position was made even worse when the patient coughed causing loops of small intestine to protrude from the gaping incision. After repeated attempts to impress upon the patient that he really must try and relax and keep still and not cough, and despite further injections of local anaesthetic the position still remained the same. At this point Mr. Hill completely lost his temper, and delivered himself of the following tirade: "If you don't wish your guts to be put back where they came from, don't think I want to put them back. I am simply doing it for you. Mine are perfectly in place. As you are not behaving as though you want yours where they should be, I wouldn't dream of acting against your wishes, so I am going off!" At this stage Mr. Hill, by now very red in the face, walked out of the theatre, to the consternation of all. I placed a pack over the wound covering the extruding bowel, and a nurse did her best to pacify the patient who by this time, did not know what was going to happen next. It must have been a much worse experience than any he had experienced at sea even in the fiercest storms. After a few minutes however, Mr. Hill returned, having calmed down considerably, and with further trials and tribulations the wound was eventually stitched up and the operation successfully completed. Mr. Hill, as was his invariable custom, thanked the staff as he left the theatre and appeared to have fully recovered from his unseemly behaviour. He was one of the few surgeons who never failed at the end of his operating sessions to make a special point of thanking the staff, whatever his mood.

When the sailor was back in the ward I spent some time telling him how fortunate he had been to have such a brilliant surgeon to do his operation, and the reasons for his not having been put to sleep, chiefly on account of his chest. I went on to explain that while perhaps Mr. Hill had a rather bluff manner, he really did not always mean what he said.

If operations performed by Mr. Hill under local anaesthesia produced some highly charged situations, neither were the more commonly used general anaesthetics spared his eruptions. As a house surgeon I did not have to administer anaesthetics as I had at my last appointment, but at the end of my six months I applied for and was appointed to the post of resident anaesthetist, always known as the R. A., and during this time came into contact with all the surgical staff.

Mr. Hill was by far and away the most nerve racking surgeon to anaesthetise for, being as always too ready to complain. As I have already explained, the techniques available then were pretty basic, and inductions of full anaesthesia could be, at times, an unpleasant and lengthy procedure. When this happened there was inevitably a delay before the patient could be wheeled into the operating theatre. On these occasions, if Mr. Hill was the surgeon, he would repeatedly look through the glass window of the anaesthetic room with an expression of exasperation, and would sometimes send in a nurse to enquire what was the cause of all the unnecessary hold up. And if in one of his really bad moods, he would ask if he would have time to go down to see a case in the ward. Or sometimes he would send a nurse to tell the anaesthetist on no account to hurry as he was perfectly willing to spend the rest of the day waiting for the patient to be put under.

Mr. Hill liked his patients deeply anaesthetised as this afforded much greater ease of operating; he was intolerant of inadequate muscle relaxation, and was not slow to voice his displeasure. I can recall an occasion when I was giving an anaesthetic to a well built young man suffering from acute appendicitis. Knowing he would need to be fully relaxed, and the more so as the surgeon was Mr. Hill, I deepened the anaesthetic to what I considered to be the ultimate point of safety. Soon after the incision into the abdominal wall had been made, the patient's breathing became very shallow and all but ceased; this was clear evidence of too deep a stage of anaesthesia. I at once removed the ether soaked mask from the face, and waited for the depth to lighten. For what seemed an age, but must only have been a matter of minutes at the most, the respirations were barely perceptible. I was about to pluck up courage to ask Mr. Hill if he would cease operating and press on the chest to start the patient breathing again, (in the old days this was by no means a very uncommon request) when to my great relief normal respirations started of their own accord, and then I had all quickly under control. Knowing the patient would be fully relaxed, enabling the surgeon to work under ideal conditions, I thought I should draw Mr. Hill's attention to my excellent anaesthetic, so I enquired if everything was all right. To my great surprise, back came the answer, "Splendid thank you, I'm just stitching up the skin!" The operation for the removal of an acutely inflamed appendix had taken only five minutes from start to finish. It had been a perfectly straightforward case, deeply relaxed. I had been so concerned at what was happening at my end, the top, that I had not been aware of the speed at which the appendix was being removed. Mr. Hill was most decidedly quick, not only in operating but in temper also.

Intravenous anaesthesia was just starting to come into use whilst I was resident anaesthetist. It offered great advantages in place of the unpleasant and at times alarming inhalation inductions, necessitating holding a mask over the face, unconsciousness could be produced by an injection of a drug into a vein in the arm - initially Evipan was used but later was replaced by Pentothal. This was an enormous advance, for patients had no longer to fear an anaesthetic; it was completely free of any unpleasant sensations, and above all there was no mask clamped over the face, with the accompanying feeling of impending suffocation.

However, there were dangers associated with this newly introduced intravenous technique, and as in so many new advances perhaps initially they were not fully appreciated. The older general practitioner anaesthetists - specialists in this developing field were still the exception and not the rule - were wary of this new drug and argued that once it had been injected into a vein it was in the general circulation and you couldn't get it out again; whereas if you had overdone the amount of ether, you could always remove the mask from the patient's face. They were correct in stressing the dangers at this early stage of intravenous anaesthesia, and unfortunately a few disasters occurred before these were properly understood.

Towards the end of my R.A. appointment I was required to give an anaesthetic to one of the house surgeons who had to undergo an emergency operation, and was most anxious not to be submitted to the usual inhalation procedure with gas or ether, for he feared the thought of having a mask placed over his face. After considerable persuasion, I reluctantly agreed to induce him with an intravenous injection of the relatively new drug Evipan. It so happened that Mr. Hill was in the theatre unit prior to the start of the operation, though he was not performing this particular one. With hindsight I foolishly mentioned to Mr. Hill that I was about to give Evipan to a fellow resident. He reacted violently to this, as he did on so many occasions.

"Good God!" cried Mr. Hill in alarm. "You will kill the man, I had better go and say good-bye." So saying he marched into the anaesthetic room where the H.S. nervously waited on a trolley, and putting out his hand briskly remarked, " I hear you are going to be given Evipan so I have come to wish you good luck. I must say you are a braver man than I am. I hope nothing goes wrong, but if it does you won't know anything about it. Good-bye, should I not see you again!" He then withdrew in the manner of one leaving a death bed This uncalled for charade before starting the anaesthetic did nothing to enhance my confidence nor, I am sure, that of the patient. However, all went well and the house surgeon came to in the lift on the way back to the ward to find the matron stroking his forehead.

These anaesthetic experiences which I have mentioned were to follow the conclusion of my six months as a house surgeon; I have written them at this stage as they fit in so well with of Mr. Hill's image as a surgeon.

Chapter Fourteen

If Mr. Hill could be a tiger in the theatre he was certainly no lamb in the ward. I never knew, when doing a round, what would happen next. One afternoon he was in a particularly foul mood and excelled himself even by his bad tempered standards. A few of the patients had certainly been a little difficult, and the atmosphere was becoming even more tense as we progressed along the beds, for nothing seemed to be right. The climax came when the round stopped at the bed occupied by a fattish woman who gave every appearance of enjoying her stay in hospital and being a centre of interest. When asked by Mr. Hill what was the matter she replied in a querulous voice, "My insides felt all like a jelly," and having made this effort sank wearily back on her pillows, giving the impression of utter exhaustion. She was quite taken aback when Mr. Hill replied, "I don't treat jellies so you can go home this afternoon." After this profound announcement he moved on to the next bed. Following this episode all went well for a while, and the round was coming to an end when, at the very last bed, a patient recently admitted for investigation, was asked what she was complaining of. Thinking she should make light of her symptoms, thus hoping to establish herself as a patient who seldom, if ever, complains, replied engagingly, "I really feel quite a fraud lying here, I haven't any pain today."

"Perfectly splendid!" came Mr. Hill's retort. "Then in that case you can go home!"

After the round, the chief having been suitably conducted off the ward, Sister would go and see any of the patients who had been upset and explain that Mr. Hill did not really mean what he said, it was just his manner, though she did understand that if not used to his ways it could be a little upsetting. She always finished by telling them they were indeed fortunate to be under the care of such a clever surgeon. If a patient had been more than usually upset, I would return to the ward after I had conducted Mr. Hill to the main entrances and do my level best to come to the aid of the sister. Ward rounds were not always marred with upsets, often all would proceed smoothly and pleasantly, for Mr. Hill could be as charming as he could be bordering on the impossible. You never knew, however, what was coming next; his moods changed so rapidly, one small omission could change sunshine into darkness. Of all his outbursts, the most unforgivable happened to a patient with an infected knee.

This poor man, in early middle age, had been in hospital for some weeks with a severe infection of his knee joint, and had already had two operations in an attempt to drain the pus; but despite these efforts the infection continued to spread. In the pre-antibiotic era, sepsis of this nature was always a serious danger. Mr. Hill considered that as the patient was becoming increasingly more toxic, and was deteriorating quite rapidly, there was no other course open but to amputate the leg through the middle of the thigh. Accordingly, and with no attempt at explanation, Mr. Hill announced to the ill and distressed patient, "I am going to take your leg off this afternoon." Naturally the wretched man was completely taken aback and utterly shattered at this dreadful prospect, and not surprisingly replied, in an agonised voice, "Oh no, Doctor, please not that. I've had two operations already, and I don't feel I can go through with any more, and please, not my leg." Quite unmoved, Mr. Hill exclaimed,

"Don't think I want to take your leg off; I'm doing it for your sake. My leg is quite all right; don't run away with the idea I want to go round cutting legs off." Having delivered these devastating words, he turned away from the patient and left the side ward - being very ill he was in a room to himself. Mr. Hill barely had time to close the door before he was back, and standing some little distance from the patient, asked him for the name and address of his general practitioner, and on being told who he was said, "I will drop him a line to let him know you will be dead in three days now you have refused to have your leg off." There was a sad ending to this sordid tale. After sister and I had explained the position with all the sympathy and understanding at our command, the patient eventually decided to sacrifice his leg for his life, but despite the amputation the infection continued to progress and he died of septicaemia. With antibiotics his life and indeed his leg could have been saved.

Despite Mr. Hill's difficult temperament I got on well with my chief, and he for his part, with few exceptions, treated me almost as an equal. I was always at great pains to have all my work and case notes up to date and to make certain I knew everything I possibly could about his patients, as under no circumstances whatsoever would he tolerate slackness and inefficiency. As I have already mentioned, Mr. Hill was a curious mixture. At times he could be kind and thoughtful, at other times quite the opposite, and always completely unpredictable; if he took an instant dislike to someone, that was it, and his mind, once made up, was never changed. He once told me how he came to plough a candidate in an oral examination. I quote:

"When the man came into the room I could see he had made up his mind that I was out to fail him. As I didn't see why I should disappoint the fellow, I did just that. He will get through next time and should have made it this time if he hadn't been so stupid!"

Though by no means popular with his fellow Honoraries, Mr. Hill was tolerated, being regarded as one of the hospital's characters and looked upon as a fine surgeon. Surprisingly, neither was he altogether unpopular with the nurses, despite the all too frequent outbursts of temper. It amazed me how he got away as he did with some of his worst tantrums, but everything was so very different over fifty years ago, being in some ways a much tougher world. The patients, on occasions, certainly had to have considerable stamina. One morning I was summoned to the out-patient department to see a man, whom Mr. Hill requested me to circumcise as an out-patient under local anaesthetic. As he put it: "The chap is getting married in six weeks' time and wants to be put in working order for the honeymoon." Now, being circumcised as an adult under a local is not a very pleasant experience, especially if the operator is a mere H.S., and being done as an O-P. is by no means the ideal way. I had performed only a very few adult circumcisions, and these under a general anaesthetic as in-patients. It was therefore with certain reservations that I embarked on the operation. I felt the patient might well be embarrassed lying fully displayed on the operating table with a spot light focused on his organ, and in the presence of a nurse who was assisting, with the instruments. Fortunately he was nicely equipped, for nothing so embarrasses a man as to 'be small made'.

Considering the operation was being performed under local anaesthesia the patient behaved remarkably well; clipping and tying off the severed blood vessels can be a painful procedure, but on this occasion there was no undue complaint, and despite the presence of an attractive nurse there was no question of arousal, for in times of stress erections seldom occur. To end up with a circumcision looking aesthetically correct is not always easy; too much skin can be excised, or on the other hand too little. But on this occasion I had fortunately judged the right amount to be removed and I felt well satisfied with my handiwork. I am sure walking home must have been a painful business for the pants and trousers could not but fail to be most uncomfortable rubbing against the so recently inflicted wound. I do not recollect his subsequent progress, one can only hope he felt it was well worth the discomfort when it came to trying it out on the wedding night. Looking back, this patient should certainly not have been allowed to walk away from the hospital without any transport, but in those days times were tough. This case has remained firmly in my mind as it was the only instance in a long surgical career when I performed an adult circumcision as an out-patient and let the patient walk home, but I was, of course, only doing what I had been told to do at the time.

Writing of this honeymoon preparation brings to mind the apocryphal story of the very young and naive bride recounting with gusto to her fellow office workers all the details of her recent wedding, and ending up by saying, "It was a wonderful day; and to make matters even more perfect I found that my husband was a virgin." When one of the girls laughingly retorted she couldn't possibly have known, she was told how wrong she was, for when it came to the night of nights his was still wrapped in cellophane.

As house surgeon to both Mr. Wansfell and Mr. Brooke Hill I was kept extremely busy, having literally no spare time except for an official half day a week, which, more often than not, I could not take on account of an accumulation of work which had to be got through before the next day. I had, however, alternate week-ends off, from Saturday after lunch until Sunday night. Apart from these official off duty times, I was on call for every hour of every day and quite often at the end of a very hard day I would be called out of bed at night for urgent cases.

Mr. Wansfell was as different as chalk from cheese when compared with Mr. Hill. I have written at some length about the latter, and little of the former, for it was Mr. Hill's erratic behaviour and childish outbursts which high-lighted my time as his H.S. although I was most fortunate in meeting with his approval, I much preferred working for Mr. Wansfell, who could not have been more helpful to me, as indeed he was to all his staff, provided they gave of their best; the patients were always his primary concern. Mr. Wansfell was a dedicated surgeon, and impressed on his juniors that the definition of a true surgeon is a doctor who operates, and never to forget, at all costs, to avoid becoming just a surgical technician. I am sure he practised what he preached, and worried if a patient on whom he had operated developed complications - he was assiduous in his attention, visiting the wards daily, more often than not coming in in the evening to assure himself all was well.

A sense of humour, however, was not amongst the many virtues of Wansfell, and he did not approve of the slightest levity in the operating theatre. The Bacillus Coli, know as the B.C.C., is a normal habitat of the large bowel, and under certain circumstances can lead to peritonitis. Mr. Wansfell was operating on a patient for acute appendicitis, and finding turbid fluid in the peritoneal cavity and fearing the early onset of peritonitis, obtained a sample of the fluid, by means of a sterile swab held on a stick, and, asking a nurse to lower his face mask, took a strong sniff at the swab, before announcing, "I can smell the B.B.C., that's a bad business." He had no idea that he had meant to say the B.C.C. and not the B.B.C. and could not understand my ill disguised difficulty in attempting to keep a straight face.

If I was somewhat embarrassed, my feelings were as nothing to those of a fellow house surgeon whilst assisting his chief with an emergency operation. As the abdomen was being opened, at this crucial stage, he unwittingly let off a silent malodorous fart, the kind known, I believe, as a cushion creeper. As the odour permeated to where the surgeon was standing, he naturally assumed it was arising from the operation site and announced that he thought there must be a perforation of the bowel to account for the smell. The H.S. was too embarrassed to explain he was the culprit, and felt exceedingly uncomfortable as the whole of the intestine was carefully examined to exclude a perforation, with, of course, negative findings. Surely this was a practical demonstration, which the H.S. would willingly have foregone, of the conundrum asking, "Do you know what the stomach said to the belch?"

"If you keep quiet I will let you out at the back."

With Mr. Wansfell I gained considerable operative experience, whereas Mr. Hill was far too impatient to assist and instruct. He usually ended up doing the operation himself, remarking that perhaps he had better take over whilst the patient was still alive. Mr.

Wansfell was very different and I enjoyed operating with his assistance, he was patient and understanding, and as a result I gained confidence under his kindly guidance.

One day, to my surprise, he said, "You do this appendix with the help of sister. I am not going to scrub up, but will be in the theatre unit if you want any help." This was to be the very first time I had opened an abdomen without an experienced surgeon to assist me. Initially, I was a little nervous at the thought, and my hand was none too steady when I came to make the incision. But after I had been operating for a few minutes, my confidence returned, and as the operation progressed I felt much more at ease. From time to time my chief looked over my shoulder to check that all was well. When the time came to stitch up the skin incision, a warm glow of satisfaction welled up inside me, for unaided by another surgeon, I had successfully completed my first abdominal operation, and moreover Mr. Wansfell said that it had been nicely done; this was heartening as I greatly valued his opinion. I was to discover later on as I progressed up the surgical ladder that there is all the difference in the world between operating alone with an experienced surgeon at hand if in difficulties, as opposed to being without expert help, when it is 'all up to you'.

I think it was from now on that I began to think seriously of my medical future, and I was coming more and more to the conclusion that I wanted to specialise in one branch or another so that I could really be on top of the job. Although my original intention had been to enter general practice, my time as a hospital resident was gradually but steadily changing my ideas, for it seemed to me the field of general practice was so wide it would be next to impossible to be an all round expert, and I wished to be an expert at something. The adage that a GP knows less and less about more and more, and the specialist more and more about less and less, has a modicum of truth, and though perhaps unfair to the practitioner, aptly summed up my feelings at the time. Very largely due to the influence and encouragement of Mr. Wansfell I was fast leaning towards a surgical career, though I realised fully that this would mean a hard slog for some years, and entail taking the F.R.C.S. examination, which was an absolute pre-requisite to obtaining the ultimate goal of a consultant surgeon. In the mean time I had to complete my resident hospital appointments, and although I was worked hard, exceedingly so at times, I was enjoying my days tremendously, a delightful change of circumstances when compared with earlier times.

Chapter Fifteen

When it came to calling my chiefs out for emergency cases, again there was a different reaction from Mr. Wansfell and Mr. Hill. Mr. Wansfell always came without demur whatever the hour. He had an unusual way of answering the phone, for when it rang he invariably lifted the receiver and asked, "Are you there?" He didn't drive himself, and if it was late at night he used not to disturb his chauffeur, coming to the hospital on a bicycle which he mounted by use of a step on the back wheel. In the olden days this was the accepted practice for the gentlemen 'to get into the saddle'. At first it struck me as rather incongruous to see the senior surgeon cycling to the hospital, and still more so when, on occasions, he was wearing evening dress; but he took it all in his stride, and never once complained at being disturbed.

Mr. Hill however, was not so accommodating, especially if disturbed at night. From time to time an acute abdominal emergency would be admitted. Not being too certain as to the diagnosis I would phone Mr. Hill, and after the usual apologies for disturbing him in the early hours of the morning, would briefly outline the salient points of the problem, and conclude by saying, "I would very much appreciate your opinion, Sir, whether or not the abdomen should be explored." The conversation would proceed as follows:

Mr. Hill: Do you want me to operate ?

Me: I would like you to see the case first, Sir, as I cannot be sure of the diagnosis.

Mr. Hill: (Impatiently) I said, do you want me to operate or not? If I come I shall operate, if I don't come I shan't operate.

Me: (By now not knowing what to say next, but determined to press my point) I would very much like you to see the case first, please, Sir.

Mr. Hill: Very well then, get the theatre ready in half an hour.

At the time about which I am writing, there was no senior resident surgeon who could operate on emergency cases. The four surgical

Honoraries took it in turns to be on call, and taken all round they served the hospital well, working hard and giving freely of their services. With but very few exceptions the patients were consistently treated with kindness and consideration. As in all hospitals, especially in the years long past, there were inevitably the odd characters.

There was the gynaecologist, for instance, who rather fancied himself as a man for the girls, and insisted on having the most attractive nurse in the theatre constantly in attendance by his side, to mop his brow whilst operating. He had a tendency to sweat profusely; if, on turning away from the patient to have a mop, the nurse was not there, he demanded to know where his little 'ray of sunshine' had gone. He was always correct in his remarks in front of the nursing staff, but to his H.S., he used to allude to the anatomy of the female perineum as 'the pleasure ground at the front, and the sewage works at the rear'.

Then there was one of the Honorary physicians, a Dr. Wootton, a likeable eccentric bachelor getting on in years. He lived with his maiden sister in a large house some miles from the hospital, and without fail, arrived on a motor cycle wearing, whatever the weather, leather helmet and oil skins, which the residents alluded to as 'Dr. Wootton's sewage kit'. His gardener started the motor-bike for him on leaving home, and the head porter did the same for the return journey. Somehow Dr. Wootton didn't appear to like the idea of starting it himself. It was quite a ceremony when he was ready to leave, with the porter wheeling the machine to the front entrance and ceremoniously starting up the noisy engine before handing the motor to the waiting Dr. Wootton, already garbed in his sewage gear. He was no speed merchant, and set off at a dignified pace down the driveway.

It was Dr. Wootton's custom to invite his house physician, shortly after taking up his appointment, to lunch on a Sunday, and, with instructions as to the best way to get there, the H.P. was told to come early. This invitation appeared to offer the prospect of a drink, or possibly drinks before luncheon, a slap up meal and a welcome opportunity to get to know his chief, and hopefully of creating a good impression. Accordingly dressed in an immaculate suit, when the Sunday dawned off went the H.P. to the lunch date with his chief. On arrival, he was informed that Dr. Wootton was digging in the vegetable garden and left a message would he go and join him. On reaching his chief, he found him dressed in a pair of old corduroy trousers and thick heavy boots, busily engaged in turning over great sods of soil in a deep sodden trench. Dr. Wootton greeted his house physician warmly, shook hands, not being the slightest bit concerned that they were caked in sticky mud, and invited him to fetch a spade and lend a hand with the digging remarking that it really was too much for one man to do on his own.

Glancing casually at his H.P.'s immaculate attire and highly polished shoes, Dr. Wootton mentioned in passing, "I say, you shouldn't have bothered to put on a suit. I forgot to tell you, I always wear old clothes on Sunday, but never mind, it's only good country mud, and once it's dry it will doubtless brush off all right!" There was no option for the now thoroughly demoralised H.P. but to join his chief in putting in some pretty strenuous digging, all the while acutely conscious of the harm being done to his shoes and suit for it was becoming increasingly clear they would be in no fit state to be worn at future interviews. It was considered essential to present yourself in a dark suit to create the right impression, and at that time few House Surgeons or Physicians could run to more than one suit.

As the trench grew deeper and the work grew harder it became increasingly more difficult to free the spade from the glutinous mud, and following a particularly bad patch when the spade all but became cemented to the clay, the by now quite dispirited H.P. was reminded of the angry farmer accusing a worker that his son had put his daughter in the family way.

"Clumsy bugger, broke a spade last week," was the only reply.

Around 1.30 p.m. to 2 o'clock Dr. Wootton suggested breaking off for something to eat. This proved to be a further disappointment as no pre-lunch drinks were offered, just a glass of beer with the meal, and when this was finished Dr. Wootton said he would welcome a helping hand in rolling the tennis court - it was rather heavy for just one man, and perhaps it was not wise to do anything too strenuous directly after lunch.

I don't imagine for one moment he meant to be inconsiderate, he just didn't stop to think, and, being an elderly bachelor, was set in his ways. On subsequent visits his H.P. knew what to expect and dressed accordingly!

Dr. Wootton was a physician of the old school, and impressed on his juniors the importance of observation, for the eyes were a great help in diagnosis, and only too often were not brought into use enough. To illustrate his point he was fond of recounting how his old chief used to place a specimen of diabetic urine on a table and tell his students that it was possible to detect diabetes by tasting the sugar, at the same time putting his finger into the urine and then into his mouth. He next passed the specimen round and insisted all followed his example; so very reluctantly each dipped a finger into the urine and then into their mouths. But there was a great difference between the chief and the students - whereas the former dipped one finger into the specimen and another into his mouth, the students used but the one finger; the penalty of faulty observation and the point tellingly made.

Dr. Wootton did not wholly approve of the decision to appoint a psychologist to the staff, for the speciality was then in its earliest days, and was not really taken very seriously. He considered that a good all round general physician with sound common sense could cope with most of the problems and he had managed all his time without their help. The Honorary appointed was a nice enough man but was not very popular on account of his patients; the hospital being chronically short of beds, he was allocated only a few in a general ward, which proved to be a most unsatisfactory arrangement, and was most certainly a mistake. As was only to be expected it gave rise to some awkward situations. On one occasion I received an urgent call to the ward by a highly indignant sister (who naturally resented these peculiar patients disrupting her previously well organised ward) for one of the patients had left her own bed and climbed into bed with another patient, and declined to budge.

"Here I am and here I stay!" she repeated over and over again, "I have as much rights to this bed as anyone else and I'm sticking to my rights." Unfortunately, the patient selected as her bed mate was too ill to move, and it was not an easy problem to solve. On another occasion, a patient left her bed and took up her abode under another patient's bed and again refused to move saying she felt more secure with someone on top of her. Trying to dislodge a disorientated patient from under someone else's bed without upsetting the whole ward was no easy matter, and naturally enough the rest of the patients viewed these episodes with foreboding, and the nurses found it all most unsatisfactory. It was not long before alternative arrangements had to be made. There were not the drugs then which are now available to treat these unfortunate individuals; had there been, these and other disturbing incidents could have been avoided.

Despite the very occasional disturbances to the routine, the patients were extremely well cared for, and the hospital was blessed with a first rate nursing staff, who were truly dedicated young women. In those days there was never any question of a shortage of nurses, on the contrary, there was a lengthy waiting list. As in all large hospitals of the period, discipline was strict, and Matron came down heavily on any misdemeanour. The year before I arrived, the Christmas Dance, held in the out-patient hall and attended by the nursing staff, residents and Honoraries, and greatly looked forward to as the most enjoyable event of the festive season, had been brought to an abrupt end. Normally it did not finish till one in the morning, or possibly even later if Matron was enjoying herself and could be cajoled into asking the band for an extension. On this occasion, a couple of resident doctors had been discovered in the nurses' home, a truly heinous offence! Presumably they had reasoned that it would be a good time to pay a visit, thinking all the sisters would be enjoying themselves at the dance, and they would be in the clear; but unfortunately this was not the case, for they were spotted, by the home sister who had remained on duty. She at once reported the matter to Matron who, on being told what had happened, with no more ado, went up to the band and told them to play 'God Save the King' even though it was barely eleven o'clock, and that was the end of the dance.

Home sisters of former times guarded their nurses as a hen guards her chicks, and kept a tag on all their activities, especially when it came to being back in the home at night at the right time. Late passes were strictly limited and even then did not extend beyond eleven p.m. and often only till 10.30. Small wonder the home sister was often looked upon as a kind of bogey, and all manner of devices were thought up to circumvent the curfew.

Later on, when I moved to another large hospital, I met a home sister who showed considerable originality when it came to seeing all her flock were safely in. The nurses fortunate enough to have ground floor rooms were able to enter through the window, thus avoiding the regulation door. In the event of the sister carrying out spot checks to see if they were in bed, it was not very difficult to arrange the pillows so that it appeared they were indeed asleep. A certain nurse was making regular habit of this subterfuge, and the home sister, becoming suspicious, took extra care to check and was rewarded by discovering the bulge beneath the clothes was not the body of a nurse, but merely bundles of pillows positioned in such a way as to represent her person. Sister, more than pleased with herself, removed the pillows and, slipping on a dressing gown, got into bed herself and waited for the nurse to climb in through the window. When she finally appeared, having enjoyed a night out on the tiles, she had a most unpleasant surprise to find her pillow arrangement had turned into a full blown home sister.

Chapter Sixteen

'The residents' night rounds were looked upon with grave suspicion by the senior night sister. Apart from professional discussions, she did not approve of any friendly little 'chats' with the nurse; though these certainly were the rule rather than the exception. Normally, the nurse or nurses, would know approximately at what time one or other of the sisters was due on the ward, though occasionally they could be caught out by an unexpected visit. A light sprinkling of granulated sugar over the floor leading off the corridor to the ward served to give additional warning of the approaching danger, for the sister's shoes treading on the sugar would be clearly audible. Despite as much supervision as the night sisters could manage, the night rounds were as a general rule, looked forward to by the resident doctors, each having their own favourites, and opportunities were made, after the patients' needs had been seen to, for a little relaxation between the doctor and the nurse. It was, at the time, the custom to evaluate the nurses in terms of body units - B. U.'s for short; the highest figure being plus 10, and the lowest minus 10. Points were awarded on the basis of the usual statistics, together with the individual all round attractions. Very few ever obtained the highest mark of 10. This system was thought to be a rough guide and a help if anyone had not met a particular nurse who might be under discussion. To the question of 'what's she like?' the reply would come back, "Not at all bad, plus 5 or even possibly 6." Sometimes the points were given on the minus side. I am sure we fully appreciated that a minus 10 was as good a nurse, and often even better, than a plus 10, but perhaps not when it came to the night rounds. Occasionally, after a change over of the night staff, which occurred every three months, the fortunate H.P. or H.S. would find an absolute cracker on one of his wards. The first night of duty was always of extra interest to the residents, who wondered if they would be up or down on the B.U.'s. It would have been interesting to know if the nurses had a similar grading for the doctors; they probably had though possibly using different criteria.

There was certainly a story going the rounds of a come-hither nurse, to say the least not suffering from hypothermia, who had been 'dating' an H.P. for some time, and considered that he was being very slow off the mark. When, at last, he really got down to hard facts, she was bitterly disappointed with his showing; she is said to have told her closest friend it was no bigger than a 'winkle picker'!

Although still sexually inexperienced I was now beginning to take some interest in the physical attractions of the nurses, though this went no further than mild petting and occasionally a light smack on an attractive bottom. Years later I read in a book that men prefer girls with small round bottoms as opposed to small flat ones; but in those days I was far too immature to appreciate the finer points. As with the rest of my fellow house physicians or surgeons, I had my favourite night nurse and I always left her ward to the last. I have no recollection of her position on the B.U. scale, but I do remember I enjoyed talking to her after we had settled all the patients.

One evening, whilst turning over some notes, I chanced to see a pathological report which started off by saying that the tumour was the size of a walnut. This reminded me of an amusing tale concerning a surgeon at my medical school which I proceeded to relate. This particular surgeon was always most upset if we, as students, described the size of a tumour in terms of eggs, oranges, walnuts, etc. He never failed to point out that this was most unscientific - the only accurate measurement was in terms of inches or centimetres, which was always consistent, whereas the size of an orange, for example, depended on the orange. After one of his students qualified and settled in general practice, with tongue in cheek, he referred a patient to his former chief, and in the letter of introduction described the tumour as the size of the yolk of a poached egg. Back came the reply from the specialist saying he fully concurred with the diagnosis, though he most certainly did not agree with the stated tumour dimension, for this, in his opinion, was not the size of the yolk of a poached egg, on the contrary, he considered it to be the size of a 'piece of a banana'. I had just finished recounting this anecdote, and was sitting at the desk not writing any case notes, when the senior sister paid one of her unexpected spot checks. Finding me sitting down, obviously gossiping, to the nurse in charge, she demanded to know what I was doing.

"Nurse," she added, "has far too much to do to waste her time talking to you!" There happened to be, on the desk, a vase of roses, and on the spur of the moment I explained to the sister that I had been likening the flowers, smelling so sweetly, to the stages a student nurse goes through in the course of her training.

"This," said I, pointing to a bud not yet open, "represents the first year nurse whose vision of the future is as yet unseen. This bud now beginning to open its petals and develop its own characteristics and charm, is the second year student. And this," I concluded warming to my subject and pointing to a rose in full bloom, "is the nurse in all her fragrance."

"Indeed," retorted sister, coldly, "and now will you please tell me which of the roses is supposed to be night sister?" I'm afraid my reply was anything but gentlemanly as I told her, "I'm afraid you will have to wait a day or two for the blooms to fade a little before I can show you!" Needless to say, I should not have made such an ungallant remark, and would not have done so had I been socially more mature. I have no idea what sister said to the nurse, for I then left the ward, leaving behind me, I fear, a highly charged atmosphere.

If I was naive at this period of my life, some nurses were no more experienced. In those far off days, girls lived a more protected life and were not so obviously sex-oriented. They were also, and with every justification, terrified of becoming pregnant. Legal abortions were decades in the future, and birth control methods primitive and often ill understood; all this was so very different from the present. It was not considered done to discuss sex or birth control procedures in public; it was all somewhat hush hush, and if an unfortunate 'accident' occurred it tended to be swept under the carpet. Sex was looked upon, by the older generation, as something rather shameful; today it is quite the opposite, and is freely and openly discussed.

A few years ago a wag pinned a notice up in the dining room of a large hospital announcing that a meeting of all the virgins on the nursing staff would be held at 9 o'clock in the telephone kiosk. Apart from the notice being removed just as soon as it was spotted by the authorities no action was taken; whereas in the early 30's it would most certainly have created a rumpus.

Naive as I was, at least one nurse was even more unworldly and could have had no experience whatsoever of the opposite sex, still less of their outpourings. She had, on her ward, a male patient, who had been admitted for investigations for P.U.O. - pyrexia of unknown origin. All the usual string of tests had been done but still the diagnosis lay in doubt. One night, when Sister was doing the rounds, the nurse told her, barely able to withhold a note of triumph in her voice, that she thought she had found out what was the matter with the patient.

"I think," she said, "he has Sy!" At that time syphilis was considered to be such a dread disease (and it is still a far from pleasant one) one shrank from mouthing the complete word Syphilis, somehow or other Sy didn't sound so sinister.

"What makes you say that, Nurse?" asked Sister with some perplexity.

"Well," replied the nurse, by now not a little embarrassed, "when he woke up I went to change his pyjamas as he was sweating such a lot; I found the front of his trousers was covered with a white slimy discharge!" I wonder how the sister explained the difference between Sy and a normal wet dream! Perhaps she didn't - knowing the sister she would probably dismiss it as nonsense, to the chagrin of the poor nurse.

This night sister, the senior, although a strict disciplinarian, was efficient and well able to cope with any emergency. I was awakened one night out of a deep sleep by an agitated nurse asking me to come to her ward. When I got there I found sister as usual in command. She told me that one of my patients, who was having radium treatment for cancer of the cervix, whilst using a bedpan, had apparently lost a radium implant - she was quite sure, she had felt something come away. Unfortunately the bedpan had been emptied down the ward sluice before the patient mentioned this to the nurse. The probable loss of a tube of radium was a very serious matter and caused great concern. In the early thirties, there were no such sophisticated instruments as Geiger counters to help in the search. Though it seemed more than likely that the expensive and potentially dangerous radium had disappeared down the drain, it was vital to make sure it was not in or around the bed, so a thorough and meticulous search was organised by the night sister - the bed clothes being gone over almost inch by inch, in the hope that it might be located. Thankfully, the missing tube was eventually found embedded in a fold of a draw sheet, much to everyone's relief. It must have escaped whilst the patient was getting off the bedpan. With great relief the radium was taken away and placed in a lead container, and the patient given much needed reassurance - it would be a simple matter to replace the tube in the morning.

I was never completely happy handling radium tubes and needles. We were provided with no protection apart from a small lead shield which we were expected to stand behind to protect our genitals. The radium had to be placed into small rubber tubes and then retained in position by sutures. I feared for my hands more than the possible damage to my gonads. As we only held the post of house surgeon for a six month period, and by no means handled radium every day, I presume it was considered too short a time for a real risk of radiation exposure, but I am quite sure it would not have been allowed now.

Not very long after the bedpan scare, I had a second episode to do with this much maligned utensil. A well proportioned woman had been admitted to the ward for an operation for gallstones, and as was routine at this time had been given a pre-operative enema. Immediately afterwards the patient told the nurse she felt greatly relieved as now she had passed her stones there would surely be no need for her to have an operation. When asked why she thought she had passed stones she replied, "I have no doubt about it, at all, I distinctly heard them go ping in the pan!" Small gallstones can, and indeed sometimes are, passed through the bowel, but they do not all come away, others remain in the gall bladder, so an operation is still required. I explained this as simply as I could, at the time fully appreciating the disappointment of the patient who had hoped to have escaped the surgeon's knife. The House Surgeon plays a most important role in helping patients over the many anxieties which are associated with admission to hospital, and especially in a long and protracted illness.

Taken as a whole the residents got on well with both the day and night nursing staff, and the vast majority of the sisters were pleasant and helpful. Although we had to work long hours it was a happy resident's mess, we were well fed and the Honoraries treated us as responsible doctors and not just as a pair of hands.

As was to be expected, there was, at times, some harmless and friendly horse play. One morning, emerging from my bath with just a towel round my waist, I was seized by a couple of stalwart residents who proceeded to carry me down to the ward below, (the doctors' quarters were situated on top of a ward block) and ripping off the towel, they left me, absolutely starkers, at the entrance to a female ward. I had to beat a hasty retreat and take refuge in the nearest linen cupboard and call for urgent help. Another ploy was to put a cork, or even a small potato, into the end of the exhaust pipe of a resident's car and watch from afar the owner's vain attempts to start the engine - it would run for a few seconds only, and then stop. After a suitable interval someone would offer their assistance and be most surprised to find an obstruction up the exhaust pipe causing the trouble, and perhaps remark that it was a funny place to keep a potato. Not all the residents, by any means, were fortunate to possess cars, and those who did were the proud owners of what would now be called clapped-out old bangers. For special occasions, wiring a kipper onto the exhaust manifold was considered a worthwhile exercise, and could be most effective as I was to find out to my cost.

I was at last, and well after the normal age, beginning to take a real interest in the opposite sex, and was increasingly attracted to the night nurse on one of my wards, spending more and more time talking to her at the end of my rounds, always with a watchful eye, should one of the sisters arrive unexpectedly. She was dark and jolly, with a trim figure, and an excellent sport - and well up on the B.U. scale. I had never before taken out a nurse but I felt I would very much like to spend an evening with Molly (that was her name) away from the hospital environs to see how we would get on in each other's company. With some hesitation I accordingly asked Molly if she would care to come out with me one night when we were both off duty, and perhaps we might go to the roller skating rink which had been recently opened and was some fifteen miles or so from the hospital. To my relief she said she would like to very much, but added she had never had a pair of skates on in her life.

"That's perfectly all right," I reassured her, "it's really very easy, but be sure to wear some old clothes as it's rather dirty should you take a tumble!" We fixed the date then and there, and as was usual, arranged to meet outside the hospital precincts, that being the normal routine for avoiding the prying eyes of the residents and nursing staff.

On this occasion, however, the subterfuge failed. I have no idea how this came about, as it was to be the first occasion I had taken a nurse out, I most certainly kept the date very much to myself. Presumably Molly must have told one of her friends, and the hospital grape-vine did the rest, for when the eventful evening arrived two of my fellow residents had everything well organised. I think they must have had a good idea it was my 'first time ever'. As my companion for the evening was getting into the car, there suddenly appeared from the dark wet night, two men under an umbrella and before we could take avoiding action, we were met with a blizzard of confetti.

As we drove into the country en route for the rink, I became ever more conscious of an unpleasant fishy odour, which initially I thought might possibly be coming from my passenger, for I had stressed the necessity for old clothes. As the stench became almost overpowering Molly tactfully remarked that my car had rather a fishy smell. I replied that I quite agreed and considered at first it was perhaps coming from her clothes as I had been so insistent not to wear anything but old things. Not a particularly tactful remark on our first evening together! Molly soon put me right as to this suggestion of mine, and adamantly declared she was in no way responsible. We realised then that the cause of the stink was not from inside the car, but coming from outside, somewhere in the vicinity of the engine. So we stopped and lifted the bonnet, and sure enough, there was a fat juicy kipper frying nicely on the exhaust manifold. Closer inspection revealed it had been firmly wired on, and it was far too hot to remove, furthermore it was dark and pouring with rain. There was nothing for it but to drive on despite the appalling aroma, and the sound of the frying kipper was an unwelcome reminder of the cause. Our tribulations were by no means over, for when we stopped at a hotel for dinner, we saw with dismay that we were covered with confetti, and being wet it was not easy to brush off. Indeed, when I left the lounge to go into the dining room, I saw, with consternation, an all too obvious patch of confetti on the seat of the chair I had just vacated, and Molly complained she could not get it out of her hair - and having no ring on her finger she felt more than a little embarrassed.

Apart from the confetti and the kipper incidents I am afraid I remember next to nothing of the rest of the evening, but I know we eventually managed to get to the rink; I very much doubt if we parked anywhere on the way back. Molly would have to be in at a fairly early hour, and I expect we were both a little unsure of ourselves and probably on our best behaviour. I felt it must have been only too obvious that I was truly a novice when it came to dating nurses, but Molly, I thought, would make all allowances, and she took the kipper and confetti episodes in good spirit, though she did admit to feeling uncomfortable over dinner with tell tale confetti so much in evidence.

She was a good egg.

After our first excursion together I asked her several times to come out with me again, but on each occasion she made some excuse. These refusals did nothing to boost my morale for it would seem I had something lacking, and as I was becoming more and more attracted to Molly it made me feel quite sorry for myself. However, when she announced her engagement a few weeks later to someone outside the hospital, I felt reassured, though very sorry, for I had come to like her very much, and looked forward to getting to know her even better. Though I was, for the first time in my life, really attracted to the opposite sex, I had no thought of marriage as I had made up my mind to become a surgeon, and realised all too clearly that years of hard work and sacrifice lay ahead if I were to achieve my objective. I would not be able to marry for some years even if I wished to do so.

I had been qualified eighteen months and more and was close to twenty five years of age when I had my first date, and even that was an innocuous affair; I had still to lose my virginity. With hindsight, I regret my long lost opportunities, but at the time I was happy enough, devoting all my energies to my work with very little free time, and when not on call quite often too tired to do anything but sleep. I was reminded of the way I misspent my youth when I came across a recent paper in which it was stated one's sexual prowess is now considered to be at its height between fourteen and eighteen years of age.

Chapter Seventeen

As April 1st drew near it was decided to make a really original April Fool. One of the senior sisters was justly unpopular with both the nursing and medical staff, and it was thought therefore that she would be an excellent target for this occasion. Accordingly, her post was advertised in the local press. It was a relatively easy matter to type the advertisement on Matron's headed note paper, using the type writer from her office, and a postal order looked after the cost of the insertion. The advertisement conformed to the usual wording for a sister's post, and concluded, "The successful applicant should have a pleasant disposition and be able to maintain genial relationships with the nursing and medical staff, and preferably be under the age of thirty." The reaction of this said Lady was as predicted, when her colleagues accused her of being a dark horse giving in her notice without saying a word to anyone; it was really rather a mean trick, and they would not have known about it had someone not chanced to see the advert in the local paper. (The sister who was the subject of this spurious advertisement had by no means a pleasing disposition, and was well up in years.) Naturally enough, the unfortunate sister took great exception to these remarks and angrily retorted that she had not the slightest idea what they were talking about. She most certainly had not given in her notice and moreover had no intention of doing so, and in the future would they please be more careful of their facts before spreading unfounded rumours around. But the rumours were not unfounded and when the newspaper was produced, the facts were all too clear. The aggrieved sister was as shocked as she was angry, and her colleagues heartily agreed that it was a rotten and shabby trick for Matron to advertise her post without saying a word, and a senior sister at that. Feeling no time should be lost in telling Matron exactly what she thought of her, she stormed up to the office, and, on knocking on the door, barely waited for the customary 'come in', for such was her fury. Controlling her voice with difficulty, for it was tremulous with barely suppressed rage, she began at once by saying, "I think, Matron, you might at least have had the common courtesy to inform me that you were going to advertise my post. After all the years I've given to the hospital, I consider you to have behaved disgracefully." Momentarily taken aback at this outburst, Matron, in turn getting cross, replied, "I have no idea what you are talking about, Sister. I most certainly have not advertised your post, and furthermore I have the strongest objection to this outburst of ill mannered abuse - you will kindly apologise at once." It was now that Sister played her trump card and, with a flourish, produced the newspaper from behind her apron, coldly remarking that perhaps Matron would like to see the evidence in print. This had the desired effect for Matron was completely deflated.

As was expected, this unhappy incident was viewed with considerable concern by the establishment, and a full enquiry was held to try to ascertain who had been responsible for sending such an advert to the local press, but there were no firm clues, and although naturally suspicion fell on the resident staff, in the absence of proof the committee were not able to take any disciplinary action. Although it was basically an unkind trick to play, even on April Fools day, some good came from it, for the sister in question, perhaps having had a fright over the dismissal, mended her ways and became more amenable. As was inevitable, this escapade caused quite a stir in the hospital for it very quickly got around, and the account I have given came from varying sources - in any close knit community very little is sacrosanct.

If I have given the impression that we spent our time larking about playing one prank after another this was most definitely not the case. We worked long and arduous hours both by day and by night, and on the occasions when we did not get to bed till dawn, we had nevertheless to be on duty at nine in the morning, and with the possibility of another disturbed night at the end of the day. So it was inevitable that there were periods of reaction to ease the associated strains and tensions; a healthy letting off of steam.

We were all young at the time and accepted this heavy work load without question, being only too anxious to do our utmost for the patients, and in this we had superb support from the nursing staff. When a patient died, the death was deeply felt; if in the prime of life all the more so, and there were occasions when the residents felt they had let the nursing staff down by failing to save the patient, and all their devoted labours had been to no avail. Although I had by now come face to face with many a distressing situation, I remained emotionally involved with the patients and their close relatives, for it seemed to me that this was all but inevitable if I was to continue to put myself in the place of my patients, a teaching I tried to practise. Being blessed with a vivid imagination this came easily, all too easily at times.

When death comes it is for the most part assumed that the face takes on a peaceful and even happy countenance, with perhaps a smile playing on the lips, now the troubles and tribulations of life on earth are over forever. The body rests with tranquillity. Personally I did not find it so. I saw nothing beautiful in death; to me death only meant failure, with the inevitable accompaniment of grief, and I observed no change in the facial expression. To me, the signing of a death certificate was a reminder that one day my own name would be appearing on the form, and it would cross my mind to wonder what would be the cause - a sobering thought.

I tried my utmost to show understanding and sympathy to the relatives, but when faced with death mere words cannot hope to heal the cruel wound. At times the grief stricken family had been sitting for hours on end, or even days, by the bedside of their dear ones, hoping against hope for some signs, however slight, that would indicate a change for the better. But it hadn't come. On such sad occasions, the sisters and nurses did all in their power to comfort the distraught bereaved; their kindness and devotion was admirable, but really little could be done in the face of such tragic circumstances. I was then, and have remained since, a firm admirer of the nursing profession - what better way of spending ones days helping others to regain their health, the most precious of all gifts. If 'Service to others is the rent we pay for our time on earth', the nurses most decidedly pay theirs in full measure.

Although over fifty years ago the mortality rate was considerably higher than at present very many patients left hospital fully restored to health. It was gratifying in the extreme to see a patient leaving the ward and being greeted with deep affection by their loved ones, fit and well, when only a short while ago they had been admitted with an acute illness which, if left untreated, would have meant certain death. This sight never failed to afford me much pleasure, and made the hard work and long hours all the more worthwhile.

Although with increasing experience I was slowly learning not to worry unnecessarily over the well being of the many patients placed under my care, I wanted so very much for all of them to get better, and this, I believe, led to undue anxiety. Years later, when I had become an established surgeon, if a patient died following an operation, it was my practice to explain to my Registrar and House Surgeon. It was an all too easy let out to remark,

"We had done our best!" This would almost inevitably be so, but our best had not been good enough to save the patient. The question always to be borne in mind and to be asked - could any one else have done any better? Self complacency ill becomes a surgeon.

When holding a post as house surgeon it is inevitable that from time to time an especially tragic case remains firmly imprinted on the mind. Though this particular tragedy happened half a century and more ago, I still retain a vivid picture, clear as if it were only yesterday. Tom, a boy in his early teens, and the only child of elderly parents, had undergone an abdominal operation. All was satisfactory for the first few days and his parents were greatly relieved that their only son had come through the operation safely, and were truly thankful. It took no imagination to appreciate just what their boy meant to them, his life was virtually priceless.

On the fourth post-operative day however, Tom complained of a slight stiffness in the jaw muscles, but as it didn't amount to much, no great significance was attached to the symptom, though a note was made to keep an extra careful watch on his progress. Within twenty-four hours the stiffness had increased, and in addition he had some difficulty in opening the jaw fully. Although otherwise progressing satisfactorily from the operation the possibility of tetanus had to be seriously considered at this stage. Unhappily, before much longer, the diagnosis became only too alarmingly clear with the onset of the dreaded spasms, which had been preceded as always with stiffness and an inability to open the jaw, hence the reason why tetanus got its name of 'Lock Jaw'.

Despite the accepted treatment at the time of enormous doses of intra-venous tetanus serum, the spasms continued with ever increasing severity, and were fearsome to behold. I had not previously seen a case of tetanus and I found the whole situation disturbing in the extreme. As even the slightest stimulation immediately produced a spasm, Tom was nursed in a side ward, with drawn curtains, and every care taken to avoid the slightest noise. Even so the terrible spasms came at ever decreasing intervals as the frightful disease relentlessly progressed. As the ill boy began to experience the muscles starting to contract again, he would be seized with dreadful apprehension as the terrible contraction mounted to a climax. At the height of a spasm the only part of him left on the mattress were the back of the head and the ankles, the body itself being arched up by the strength of the contraction and lifted some little distance from the bed. The normal healthy colour of the face and neck became a suffused blue as the respirations were temporarily arrested. After the attack had passed off, Tom would fall back on the bed utterly exhausted, only too soon to cry out in terror,

"It's coming on again!" And the ghastly process would be repeated with ever increasing intensity. In those distant days tetanus was nearly always fatal, and though massive doses of serum were administered, it was not really very effective. The modern techniques whereby the spasms can be relieved and the majority of cases cured, was well into the future. As things were at that time, although given all the drugs currently available, Tom got steadily worse and it was only too painfully clear that he was going to die. His parents were beside themselves with grief and anxiety, and implored all concerned to save their son.

"You must save him," they repeated time after time, "he's all we've got, you can't let him die." It was a fearfully traumatic time, and reminded me so much of John, the patient who died at Christmas from a fractured skull. When death came to Tom it was a merciful release, for despite very large doses of sedatives, the spasms remained uncontrollable and were horrible to witness.

His father and mother sustained a mortal blow, and their lives could never be the same again. Although they had hardly left the hospital since the illness began, they were not able to stay at the bedside for long as they just could not stand the harrowing sight of their dearly loved child being constantly wracked with such cruel spasmodic attacks. As was the only natural reaction, his poor mother, beside herself with sorrow, and completely shattered, in between her sobs, kept on repeating, "I wish he had never had the operation, he would still be alive now." The poor father was too distraught to utter a word, he was fighting hard to keep back his tears; his son, so dearly prized, had gone forever, and all was utter despair.

Happily such tragedies are in the long past and this case of tetanus following an operation could not happen today. In Tom's instance, it was assumed that the infection came from catgut, a source which has, for many years, been completely eliminated. Tetanus in any form is rarely seen today, largely because the younger generation have been actively immunised, as have the majority of adults. In the very rare event of a non-immunised individual contracting tetanus, almost always from a cut, often when gardening, adequate therapeutic measures are now available for successful treatment, and the horrible spasms no longer haunt the patient.

I was more than sorry when my appointment as H.S. to Mr. Wansfell and Mr. Hill drew to a close as I had greatly enjoyed the time, and had been exceedingly happy and had learned a great deal. I had fortunately got on well with both my chiefs, despite their vastly different temperaments, and was now feeling very much more self possessed. I no longer suffered from my previous inferiority complex which, up to becoming a doctor, had dogged me through the years. Since getting qualified and being a hospital resident I had changed a very great deal, and I have no doubt it proved to be the turning point of my life. I think perhaps I may have been a more sympathetic and understanding doctor for my years, in view of my unhappy and backward start in life; be that as it may, I was now absolutely certain I was in the right profession, and was very happy in my work. I had definitely decided to go ahead and try to get my F.R.C.S. with the goal of eventually becoming a real Consulting Surgeon. Before embarking on a course for the fellowship, however, I decided to stay on and took the post of R.A. (Resident Anaesthetist). This was a far easier appointment and would allow time for study, and would also be a means of saving some money to help to pay for the course which I would have to take if I were to have a fair chance of passing the examination.

My time as R.A. passed quickly and uneventfully. Despite the fact that I was becoming increasingly more conscious of the physical attractions of the nurses, I had not ventured to ask any of them to come out with me; apart from Molly. The kipper episode was ever present in my mind. I was sorry she had become engaged - I missed her quite a lot.

When the day came to say my final farewells, I felt exceedingly sad for I was indeed sorry to be leaving. I had learned a very great deal, and all in all it had been an extremely happy period, indeed, so far, quite the happiest of my life.

Mr. Hill shook me by the hand, wished me well and assured me that I would have no trouble in passing the F.R.C.S.; in fact I would find that I knew more than the examiners and would be able to teach them a thing or two - so typical of his unbalanced statements. For his part, Mr. Wansfell gave me some worthy advice and assured me I had the makings of a good surgeon, but to avoid the risk of too close an application. On relinquishing a house officer's post it is always somewhat of an anti-climax. Whilst a resident you are in constant demand, wanted here, there, and everywhere, and if not actually wanted in person, are constantly being asked to sign this, that, or the other. You are undoubtedly an important cog in the hospital wheel. When, however, the appointment or appointments come to an end and you walk out of the hospital gates for the last time, you immediately become a nobody, no more wanted than the man in the street, and of no more importance. Furthermore, the residents' mess and the various attractions of the nursing staff are much missed. The transition is so sudden. One day you are all-important and the next a non-person. I know these were my feelings when I left, and I was to experience them again and again in the future on leaving resident posts.

Chapter Eighteen

I now had to face up to the hard grind of passing the Fellowship examination which would mean some months away from clinical work, whilst attending a post-graduate higher surgical course, in preparation for the F.R.C.S. I do not propose to dwell on this aspect of my endeavours to become a surgeon; suffice it to say that it entailed many hours of hard work. At intervals I became almost overwhelmed with the amount of knowledge a would-be successful candidate was required to know. I wondered if I could ever make the grade, and felt how true was the American aphorism 'To gain your goal requires punctilious application - the application of your pants to the seat of your chair.' There is no easy way to the F.R.C.S. it indeed calls for much application, and much sitting on chairs.

In all the examinations I had to face during my student days and afterwards with the fellowship, I was on the whole treated very fairly by the examiners. With very few exceptions they conducted themselves as gentlemen. There were just a few who adopted a rather blustering attitude. Of the two examinations in my career which I failed, it was entirely my own fault, for I did not deserve to pass. This definitely was the case at my first attempt at the F.R.C.S. as, with hindsight, I was not well enough prepared. Throughout the written papers and orals I must have been below the high pass marks demanded, and my operative surgery viva proved to be little short of disaster. I was asked what operation I would advise for a certain rare orthopaedic condition, and one, incidentally, I had never seen. Having given my answer, I was then requested to describe in detail how I would perform the procedure, which I did somewhat hesitantly for I was well out of my depth. When I had finished, the examiner next asked what the end result of the operation I had just described was likely to be and did I consider it to be a good method of treatment; or did I, on the other hand, personally consider the results to be disappointing? I foolishly replied, "On the whole not very satisfactory."

"Oh, I see," said my examiner, "that's interesting. Now tell me, when your patient, having undergone this major operation involving spending some months in plaster, complains that there is little or possibly no improvement, are you prepared to say it's really more or less what I had anticipated as the operation I have carried out, more often than not, gives poor results?" I had realised now, only too well, what a mess I had got myself into, and had no option but to reply that on second thoughts I would not advise this procedure. The examiner had doubtless been waiting for this answer, for he immediately retorted, "But you have done it, Doctor." And that was the finish. No F.R.C.S. for me this time round. However, all went differently on my second attempt when the difficult hurdle of the operative surgery viva was successfully surmounted.

The relief of passing the F.R.C.S. was tempered with the difficulty of obtaining a post as R.S.O. - Resident Surgical Officer. So many years ago, the vast majority of hospitals had only the one R.S.O. who was held responsible for the resident medical staff, and who undertook a considerable amount of surgical emergencies; having obtained his fellowship he was now embarking on his practical training. At that time, and for a considerable number of years, R.S.O.'s were required to be single, and being more or less constantly on call, residence in the hospital was thought to be essential. I applied for a number of posts at well recognised hospitals and was duly invited to attend for interview by members of the Honorary surgical staff. Usually the proceedings went well until I was asked how many major operations I had done entirely on my own. (Although as H.S. I had operated upon a number of cases, my chief had either helped me or remained in the theatre, I could all but sense the committee members saying to themselves that this man had not had enough practical experience for the job, his operative experience falling short of some of the other candidates.) Sure enough, in due course, the hospital secretary would thank me for attending the interview, and regret that on this occasion I had not been successful, though it had been a close run decision. The 'close run decision' bit was, I am sure, the stock phrase used in an effort to bolster up the morale of the rejected candidate.

When I was finally successful in obtaining a post of R.S.O. I had the good fortune to be up against a candidate who was engaged to be married. It was the common practice to enquire if the applicants were engaged, and if not, was there a chance of this in the near future. On the whole it was considered a bad thing for the young aspiring surgeon to be contemplating marriage at this stage in his career. It would be years before he could afford to marry, and in addition, an R.S.O. with the commitments of a fiancé would be far less likely always to be available; which was a prerequisite of the appointment. When it came to my turn to be asked, I told the committee that I had no intention whatsoever of becoming engaged, and I am sure this firm reply proved to be the deciding factor, for I got the job. I could now look forward to embarking on my first R.S.O. appointment, an exciting, albeit a daunting, prospect. The hospital had not previously had a resident surgical officer on its staff, and being a new departure, there arose, inevitably, some initial problems. I was once again to find that the Matron held considerable power. She took it upon herself to order all the various requirements for the two operating theatres, and it was not long before I came up against this most unsatisfactory state of affairs. I had asked for a certain strength of catgut when closing an abdominal incision, only to be informed,

"We haven't any of that number, as Matron hasn't ordered any this week." I found this most infuriating. Later on, when I had become more established, I approached the high and mighty Matron and had a high and mighty row with her, but to no avail, for I was too small a fry. I couldn't understand how the Honorary surgeons didn't complain; perhaps it was because the theatre sister seemed happy enough with this arrangement. She was a most efficient person and had been in charge for a number of years, and held considerable power in her domain. I very quickly realised as a young and inexperienced surgeon that I could not afford, under any circumstances, to pick a quarrel with this 'August Body', as almost certainly the Honorary surgeons would ask Sister what she thought of the new R.S.O. and if she considered him to be any good as a potential surgeon. (Theatre sisters are excellent judges of a surgeon's capabilities.) To offend her could well be a fatal mistake. She was essentially a nice person and certainly one hundred percent efficient.

I started off none too well. After I had operated on my first emergency case, which I felt had gone not too badly, I left the theatre and proceeded to take off my gown, cap, mask and gloves in the adjoining sluice room, well pleased with myself. At this stage Sister appeared, and told me that it was quite plain to her where I had been brought up. Thinking that she had recognised I had had the good fortune to be trained in one of the famous London hospitals, I replied with smug satisfaction, "Is it, Sister?"

"Yes," she answered, "in the gutter." I had not bothered to wash the blood off my rubber gloves before taking them off - in those days gloves were not disposable as they have been now for many years, and were used, over and over again. If the blood was left to dry and not washed off at the end of the operation whilst still fresh, it was, consequently, difficult to remove, prior to the gloves being re-sterilised. Sister was quite within her rights to pull me up for not rinsing my gloves before taking them off, though she might, perhaps, have expressed herself in a more tactful manner.

At first I found it hard to accept that the theatre sister held so much power, and that she apparently saw nothing unusual in having all her requirements ordered by Matron. In those days of the voluntary hospitals, of course, every penny had to be closely watched, and presumably it was considered, as the most senior member of the staff, Matron would see that nothing was wasted, and nothing ordered unnecessarily - it certainly wasn't!

When the theatre sister was taking a case, that is to say, handing instruments to the surgeon, threading needles and collecting swabs, she was also not above giving a helping hand to the actual operation. When the time came to close the incision, if it was on the long side, she would start stitching up at one end, leaving the surgeon to the other, all this without a word. The first time I was given a bilateral bunion operation to do on my own by one of the Honoraries, I was completely nonplussed when Sister embarked on the one foot whilst I was operating on the other. In fairness, she was most competent, and very probably was more experienced than myself, but all the same it took me all my time not to tell her to stop and confine herself to her official duties. Had I done so, in all likelihood, I would have made an enemy capable of doing an immense amount of harm. I was only too conscious of my inexperience, and appreciated that a theatre sister can be an invaluable ally. I was only too well aware of the fact that at this early stage of my surgical career I needed all the help and support I could muster if I was going to succeed.

To begin with, the Honorary surgeons, and rightly so, kept an ever watchful eye on the new R.S.O. The surgical staff consisted of three; two of the surgeons were outstandingly good, the third was a vestige of a past era, and was nearing the age of retirement. He combined surgery with a limited amount of general practice, and was a very close friend of the theatre sister - indeed it was alleged that they had been more than friends. Be that as it may, he certainly had a number of eccentricities. I was astonished when I first saw one of his more famous foibles. Whilst scrubbing up at a theatre sink prior to putting on a sterile gown and gloves, it was his inevitable habit to smoke a cigarette. When the business of scrubbing up had been completed he spat the cigarette end out into the sink, and then his mask was lifted over his mouth and nose by a nurse, and having put on gown and gloves he was then ready to start the operation. He had another and even more extraordinary eccentricity, difficult as it is to believe. In those far-away times, long before the discovery of antibiotics, it was by no means uncommon when operating on an acute abdomen, possibly not sent to hospital at an early enough stage of the illness, to find it swimming with pus, very often of a most obnoxious odour. On such an occasion this GP surgeon, the last of his generation, would call for a cigarette 'to purify the air'. This necessitated a senior nurse removing his face mask, placing a cigarette between his lips, and then lighting it, the surgeon meantime having turned away from the patient. With the cigarette drawing nicely he would then resume the operation. I was astonished at this performance and wondered how he managed to avoid the ash dropping into the wound. It never did, however, the expertise I suppose of an inveterate smoker. As was to be expected, this surgeon's technique was outmoded, and there were occasions when I considered incorrect decisions had been arrived at when it came to a choice of operative procedure.

When I was told to follow his teaching, knowing it to be wrong, I was presented with a dilemma. When I was quite certain I was right, even with my limited experience though up to date knowledge, I went my own way. Fortunately, he had but few beds and did very little work compared with the other two much younger surgeons, who were absolutely first class. They took considerable pains to teach their young and surgically raw R.S.O. and before long I was left to carry out many of the routine emergency work; I could always call on help if in difficulty. I was soon to appreciate the difference in operating with an experienced surgeon close to hand should an emergency arise, as opposed to being the only surgeon on the spot. If, for instance, profuse bleeding suddenly started, I had to learn to cope with this unexpected complication unaided, and above all to keep calm. I quickly found it was fatal for the surgeon to panic in the face of severe haemorrhage, it invariably made matters worse, though it was all too easy to do. Furthermore, the surgeon's agitation rubbed off on the assistant and staff with a knock on effect. The right approach was to give the impression that everything was under control and the operator knew just what to do, even though at times he might be inwardly greatly worried.

Despite the occasions when I felt under some strain, I was enjoying my new role, and certainly gaining, both in experience and confidence. I very much liked having increasing responsibility for the patients, and derived great satisfaction from watching those upon whom I had operated being restored to their former good health. All the hard work, spending, at times, most of the night out of bed, feeling wretchedly tired in the morning when called on to start another day's hard slog, was more than worth while including the loss of sleep, if it meant that the patients were put on the road to recovery. To me, it afforded an inner satisfaction, hard to describe in mere words, but it was there; very much so. Perhaps it was because I was doing something so worthwhile with my life after such a lamentable start, and I felt I was fast 'making good'. I was also coming to realise that the secret of happiness is to live for work and not work to live. I appreciated how fortunate I was in living for my work.

The most usual time for emergency admissions to come to the hospital was in the evening, though a fair number were admitted during the night. The day nurses went off duty at 9 p.m. when the night staff took over. I hadn't been very long in my new job as R.S.O. when the staff nurse on a surgical ward asked me one evening if she could come to the theatre and watch the operation which I was to perform on one of her patients. She should have been off duty, but went on to explain that it was so much more interesting nursing a patient if she was able to see what had actually been done. Although an unusual request, I thought at the time that she must be a very keen nurse, anxious to get on in her profession, and as her reasons appeared to be sound, I accordingly agreed. However, she continued to make these requests whenever a patient from her ward was due to go to theatre in the late evening, and I felt I could no longer accept the reasons for staying on long after the normal off duty time. With the conceit of the young, I was forced to the conclusion that this staff nurse must have developed a crush on myself, for surely there could be no other option. This conclusion was quite gratifying for after all I had not been all that long at the hospital, and had already started to make my presence felt among the nurses. Me, of all people, who had so little experience with the girls! Yes, it really was pleasing. Perhaps after all, I possessed some charm. So far as I can remember, she was quite attractive, and I was beginning to think things were shaping nicely for a date in the near future, and then came the rude awakening. One evening I had been operating on an emergency admission, and as the patient came from 'my' staff nurse's ward, she had as usual requested permission to stay on duty to watch. I was by now convinced it was not the patient she was interested in, but the young bachelor surgeon. I had finished the operation and left the theatre on this particular night, and was not expected to return, as I seldom did. But on this occasion I had left some notes behind and so unexpectedly went back to the theatre, where, very much to my surprise, I found the theatre staff nurse and 'my' ward staff nurse clasped in a loving embrace. To begin with they were so involved in passion that they failed to notice my presence. When they did, all they could do was to disentangle themselves, with obvious embarrassment, and go their separate ways. After this episode I received no further requests to watch my operations. My ego was dealt a severe blow; perhaps it was just as well for my sense of self-importance, it doubtless did me no harm being cut down to size. This was my first experience of lesbians, and I had, in my ignorance, no suspicions until I came across the two in action. I still had a great deal to learn quite apart from surgery. I subsequently found out that these two nurses were well known among their colleagues for what they were, and when they could not be together, spent their time writing love letters to each other.

There must have been, I am sure, a number of nurses of the staff only too interested in the real thing - a well fitting uniform does much to enhance the figure, but even at this stage I was not as interested as I should have been for a man of my comparatively youthful years. Accordingly I missed out, taking no active part in this aspect of hospital life. It was still to be a while before I came to appreciate what I had lost, and what opportunities I had let slip by in my youth. All that really counted as far as I was concerned at this stage was to obtain as much surgical experience as possible to the very best of my ability. I adopted the habit of getting into bed at night, always provided the hour was not too late, to go over in my mind the operations I had performed that day, step by step. If I felt I had not done as well as I thought I should have done, I would then retrace the various steps and stages, and plan how best to improve my technique for future occasions, and, hopefully, not to make the same mistake twice. Although confining my interests and ambitions almost entirely to surgery, I was not always above noticing an especially attractive nurse, and I occasionally went out with a female house surgeon; but our relationship was purely platonic and there was never any question of opening my trousers.

The theatre unit, being old and inadequately ventilated (air conditioning plants were unheard of at the time), became unbearably hot in the height of the summer and most unpleasant to work in. After one hot and prolonged session, the nurses felt that they would feel much cooler if they were to discard the usual dresses and thick black stockings, and instead wear white shorts and shirts. A deputation accordingly went to Matron to try to sell her this revolutionary though practical idea. As was only to be expected, she immediately turned down the request.

"Quite unthinkable," she said. "I've never heard of such unprofessional conduct," adding, "if I allowed you to do as you suggest, can you imagine what the surgeons would say?"

Some, I am sure, would have been all for the change. There was one particular nurse who was noted for her good figure, and doubtless she would have looked most attractive in a pair of pure white shorts, revealing the shapely curves of her buttocks and thighs in such a way no uniform dress could hope to do. Matron was correct in her decision, it would never have done. The nurses would have proved to be too eye arresting and distracting for the house surgeons, if indeed not for the surgeons, who would have welcomed the change from dresses to shorts with literally real feelings!

So long ago, the source of infections arising from the human body was not understood. Now, it is firmly established that the common organism, the staphylococcus, has, as its habitat, the nose, and to a lesser degree the perineal regions - hence the wearing of a mask over the nose, and, in some modern operating theatres, the wearing of trousers as opposed to dresses, as it has been shown, when wearing a dress, continual movements of the thighs when walking may disturb the staphylococci harbouring in the perineum, so liberating them into the general atmosphere; whereas with trousers there is less risk. In some transplant units, where stringent precautions against infection have to be taken, the nurses not only wear trouser suits, but underneath put on sterile disposable pants. So after all, the nurses were on the right track when they requested the Matron to allow them to wear shorts, but for the wrong reasons. I remember the theatre staff nurse was quite put out that she couldn't appear in shorts. She was reputed to be 'hot stuff', and I have no doubt that she would have lost no opportunities to demonstrate her very saleable wares. It was this nurse who was most persistent in asking me to let her take out an appendix, I suppose she had seen sister at work, and I am sure she would have been more than willing to give her all as an inducement. Needless to say she did not achieve her objective.

Chapter Nineteen

I had been at the hospital a few months when a notice appeared stating that the annual fire practice would take place the following week at six o'clock in the evening. Apparently, some years ago, the nurses' home had got on fire, and several nurses had narrowly escaped being trapped; after this, as the fire drill at the time was almost non-existent, it was decided that an annual exercise of fire rescue should be carried out, making the occasion as realistic as possible. When the day came, promptly at six p.m., a fire engine and accompanying tender drove up to the hospital at high speed, and before it had had time to draw up at the main entrance, a dozen stalwart firemen in full regalia jumped off and began to manhandle the hoses which, in an incredibly short time, were all set for action. To the assembled crowd, for all staff not on essential duties were expected to turn out, it was certainly impressive and reassuring should a real fire occur. The firemen now turned on the stop cock and demonstrated the full power of the hose, the force of the water causing it to writhe like an angry snake, and it required two men to control the direction, such was the force. One of the H.S.'s remarked that the stream of water gushing from the end of the hose reminded him of the old musical hall joke where a zoo attendant announced to a party watching the antics of the elephants, "All those who can't swim stand back, the elephant is about to make water." Several nurses started to laugh at this aside, but on seeing a senior sister close by who was clearly not amused, managed to turn the laugh into a mild titter. After the impressive demonstration of quelling a blazing building, the next event was to rescue a nurse from the top window of the nurses' home, which was assumed to be on fire. The supposedly trapped nurse was gallantly rescued by the means of the fireman's lift. It really looked a most realistic scene as she was carried down a turn-table ladder in the arms of her rescuer. I suspect this was the 'pièce de résistance' of the exercise for the lucky man chosen for the exercise.

It was at this stage that the hospital secretary, resplendent in blazer and white flannels, a retired army colonel, approached me as R.S.O. with the remark: "This is where you are to do your stuff, old chap."

Doing my stuff entailed jumping off the roof onto a large sheet held by a dozen firemen. I was duly conducted up to a flat roof where it was assumed there was no other means of escape except to jump. I do not suppose it was really all that high, but when faced with the prospect of launching myself, in cold blood, onto a sheet which appeared far below, was not one I particularly fancied. The situation was made worse as, without my glasses, I could see very little - I dared not jump with them on for fear they should come off in the fall and get broken. There could be no question of hesitation for all eyes were on me, and that meant practically the whole of the hospital staff. This event was undoubtedly the climax to the evening's exercise, to have shown the slightest fear would have been disastrous.

On the command 'jump', I leapt off the roof, and in no time at all was safely caught in the sheet. As I fell onto this the firemen relaxed the tension of the sheet, and I landed comfortably. The only rather unpleasant thing about the exercise was jumping off into space, but as is so often the case when facing the unknown, it proved to be less frightening than I had anticipated. Had I been trapped by an actual fire, I am sure the decision would have been so much more easily made. The secretary, I trust, considered I had held the job down in the approved style. On hearing the command to jump, given by the chief officer, my mind flashed back to my school days when the sergeant major in charge of the officers' training corps would bawl out, "Jump to it, smarten yourselves up, I won't have you coming on parade like a squad of constipated cockroaches."

As well as this redoubtable S.M. there was another one also with considerable originality, who could express his feelings with force, and who was in overall charge of the Gym. For P.T. sessions it was necessary to wear special shoes and if a boy forgot to bring his, he was liable to a punishment drill which entailed an hour's work out on the parade ground - at times picking up the double. It was therefore the custom to try to borrow a pair of gym shoes from a friend, although this practice was heavily discouraged by those in charge. To this end the Sergeant was wont to deliver a pep talk at the beginning of the term on the real dangers of borrowing other boy's shoes. In all seriousness and warming to his subject he proceeded to explain that strenuous exercises, especially when wearing rubber shoes - "draws the feet and makes them sweat." He went on to say that should a boy happen to have tuberculosis this dread infection would seep out of the feet and into the shoes, and the next person to wear them would stand a good chance of catching T.B. It was therefore most desirable that we should wear only our own shoes. So long ago, when tuberculosis was looked upon as a killer disease, I suppose we must have been impressed and perhaps even believed what we had been told. I have since wondered if this S.M. honestly believed there was an actual risk of spreading the infection in this way, or was he a good psychologist merely seeking to frighten us so we no longer borrowed our friends' shoes.

Although everyone worked hard and gave devoted attention to the patients, there were occasions, apart from the fire demonstrations, when the lighter side of life could be enjoyed. Once a year an elaborate garden fête was held in the grounds. Before the advent of the N.H.S. hospitals were totally dependent on voluntary donations and fund raising activities. The annual fête played an important role in the finances, and there was the usual anxiety about the weather, for so much depended on the weather being fine. The year I was R.S.O. the day could not have been better, and all the usual features of these events basked in a warm sunshine. There were stalls, side-shows, raffles galore, tea tents, etc., etc., and overall an air of festivity. The august person invited to open the fête was always chosen with careful consideration; apart from being a figure of some importance in the community, a good bank account was an absolute prerequisite, for he or she would be expected to spend lavishly, at least a purchase at every stall, and in addition, to hand a nice fat cheque to the chairman at the start of the proceedings. To be included in those privileged to be on the platform was visible evidence of one's standing in the local society. Anybody who was anybody made sure they were to be seen at the hospital garden party-cum-fête: "Such a worthy cause, don't you think?"

Out of all the various attractions, there were a couple of side shows which took my fancy. One was an entrance fee of one shilling to view a water otter. Having paid the admission charge, you were then taken up a flight of steps into a small enclosure, and on entering, you were confronted with an old iron kettle! The other tent had a large notice proclaiming: "This is the only free entrance in the whole show, don't fail to miss this exciting offer." On entering there was indeed nothing to pay, but you couldn't get out without giving a donation. As the chap said, "We never mentioned a free exit." In actual fact it housed a variety of interesting and original exhibits.

I must confess to a weakness when it comes to having my fortune told for I find it hard to resist. As with nearly all fêtes at this time there was the inevitable Madame Gypsy, famous for her clairvoyance, sitting invitingly at the entrance to her tent. Needless to say, I succumbed and entered. Madame Gypsy asked me to put out my hands and proceeded to say the usual trite remarks - receiving a letter, a journey across the water and so on. Then, at the end, she took hold of my right thumb, bending it back and forth apparently in deep thought. At last she let go and pronounced, "And above all you have a very generous thumb." At the conclusion of the session I asked her what her fee was. She replied, "I leave that to you." She may not have been any good as a fortune teller but she undoubtedly had the right idea as far as psychology was concerned. I have no idea how I responded but I expect I gave too generously! With the advent of state medicine these elaborate fund raising activities are of the past; a pity perhaps, in some ways, as they helped to bring all the members of the staff together in their efforts to improve the facilities for the patients, and, at the same time, served to remind all concerned how much money a hospital gobbled up each year, and how important it was not to waste the precious commodity.

Apart from surgery, I was held responsible for the good behaviour of the resident house physicians and surgeons, who expected me, in turn, to look after their welfare. The accommodation was not very luxurious, and the food at times was certainly sub-standard. As the residents were becoming increasingly restive, I felt I must take steps to try to improve matters. The opportunity seemed to have presented itself when, one Sunday morning, we were served with cold bully beef for lunch. Fortunately, a senior member of the Honorary staff happened to be in the hospital at the time, so I mentioned the dissatisfaction felt by the residents with the food, and invited him to come to our dining room and view our lunch for himself. He accordingly accompanied me to the mess, and, on seeing what was on the table exclaimed, "By Jove, you've got pressed beef, I haven't had any for ages, you are lucky. I really must ask my wife to get some for ourselves." At this he turned and left the room heading for his Rolls Royce which was doubtless taking the Honorary to a slap up lunch at home.

Although I got on well with the Honorary staff I never really hit it off with the Matron, and I am sure she was pleased when my appointment came to an end. I found it irritating in the extreme, when asking for some surgical requirement, to be told, "I'm sorry, we haven't any left, we are waiting for Matron to order some more." I finally lost my temper the day I was putting on a plaster in the casualty department and asked for a pair of rubber gloves, for plaster of Paris, if used constantly, roughens the hands. I was told the all too familiar tale, "We haven't any left till Matron lets us have some more." That did it. I stormed out of the department and rushed straight up to her comfortably furnished office, not, I believe, ever stopping to knock on the door. I cannot recall what I said, but I remember, all too clearly, losing my temper in no uncertain fashion. The first and only time in my surgical life I have done so with a Matron. I had yet to learn the wisdom of 'act not in furious passion, it's putting to sea in a storm.' I do not think my outburst did any good with regard to the improved supply of surgical materials, and it certainly didn't do our relationship any good either, which remained frigid for the remainder of my stay.

When the time comes to leave a hospital where for months you have worked hard, and made many friends, there must always be some regrets. Coming to the end of my first appointment as resident surgical officer I realised I had made many mistakes, the majority not to do with surgery. I was young and generally inexperienced at the time, and far too ready to take offence where none was intended; and my sudden bursts of temper, as with the Matron, were undignified and often uncalled for. In justification I had at all times tried my level best to put the patients' interests above all else, and when on occasions I found I was frustrated in this, I reacted too violently which was not a good thing - I had still to learn to control my emotions. On the credit side, I had gained a wealth of surgical experience, and was more than ever determined to become a surgeon, even though I realised I had set myself a hard row to shoe.

Having once held a post as R.S.O. it was not too difficult to obtain a further post, as I now had a considerable amount of experience to back my applications. I was anxious to get as wide a training as possible by working in several hospitals, and not to remain in just one place. It was not long before I was offered a similar post as R.S.O. in the South which I gladly accepted.

Chapter Twenty

When I arrived to take up my new appointment I discovered that the former R.S.O. had not been satisfactory and had left the previous day. This had been purposely arranged so there could be no danger of contaminating the new arrival. It is usual for the outgoing R.S.O. to show the incoming one the ropes and to introduce him to the staff and patients, but it was not so on this occasion. I had barely been in the hospital a couple of hours when a man with a perforated duodenal ulcer was admitted, requiring urgent surgery. When the time came to go to the theatre to start the operation, I was surprised to find the entire resident staff of six had turned up in force to watch the new R.S.O. perform his first operation at the hospital and to assess his worth. I could happily have done without this critical audience, for operating in a strange theatre, and with strange staff, for the first time, is, at its best, rather an ordeal, and especially for an aspiring young surgeon. Fortunately a perforated ulcer is not a particularly difficult procedure, being simply a matter of opening the abdomen, sucking out the escaped stomach contents from the peritoneal cavity, then locating the small hole or perforation and closing it with catgut sutures. Much to my relief the operation was straightforward, there being no complications, and at the end I felt I had acquitted myself reasonably well, and I hoped the reception committee had been suitably impressed. I must say I was somewhat put out by their presence, I think with justification. I was naturally anxious that this, my first patient, should make a smooth recovery and was a little worried, when going into the ward the next day, I saw he had draped a large white handkerchief over his head and face. I enquired of the sister what was amiss, was it perhaps a bad headache? She replied that she didn't know and had only just noticed it. Accompanied by Sister, I went up to the patient, who was in a ward of about twenty, and, gently lifting a corner of the handkerchief, asked what was the matter. In a hushed voice I was requested to go away as he was engaged in passing water. It turned out that he came from the depths of the country and was extremely shy, and having to pass water in bed without screens he found most embarrassing. To overcome this to some extent, and to show he was engaged and not to be disturbed, he apparently felt he was afforded some privacy by covering his face with his handkerchief whilst having to pump ship. I am glad to say he made a good recovery, though he remained apprehensive in the extreme of the usual nursing routine, and he continued to wear his handkerchief when about to pass water until he was able to get up and go to the loo!

On the whole, the routine was similar to my last appointment, and the majority of the Honorary staff were easy to get on with; though in all hospitals there are usually one or two characters who can be difficult at times. One such was a gynaecologist, a Mr. Richards, who was by no means popular, being considered pompous and too full of his own importance. Furthermore, he could be bad tempered in the theatre. Although it was certainly not necessary, it was his practice, on entering his ward, to position a monocle in his eye, though he never appeared to be comfortable wearing it, and indeed on one occasion it slipped out and fell to the floor. The staff nurse, anxious to retrieve the lens, and in her haste and agitation, ended up by putting her foot on it. Mr. Richards continued his dignity whilst operating. Whereas the rest of the surgeons, if they wished the stool on which they were sitting whilst carrying out certain procedures, to be altered in height by raising or lowering the metal seat, would simply ask for it to be adjusted. Not so Richards, for invariably would come the command, "Position my chair, nurse!" He had another peculiarity. Instead of asking the theatre sister for a certain instrument, for example a Spencer Wells forceps, it was his routine to say to the sister, "Try me with a Spencer Wells forceps, sister." Or again, "Try me with a retractor," and on one epic occasion he turned to sister, whilst doing a complicated operation, and suddenly announced, "Try me with a catheter." He could not understand the barely suppressed amusement at his request.

Mr. Richards was seldom called in to operate during the night, but on the rare occasions he did, it proved a trial for the night staff for they were less prepared to deal with the foibles of particular surgeons. The vast majority of the night-time emergency cases were done by myself.

I had fallen in to the habit of going to the theatre in my dressing gown and pyjamas, and then changing into the usual operating garments. The house surgeons and anaesthetists did the same. One morning, around one o'clock, Mr. Richards phoned his house surgeon, who at the time was female, and announced (he never said or told, it was always announced) that he had sent a case in and was coming to perform an emergency operation himself, and please to organise the theatre forthwith. In due course, Mr. Richards descended on the theatre immaculately dressed as ever, to be met with his H.S. wearing a dressing gown partially covering a glamorous nightie, the sight of which had the same effect as the proverbial red rag to a bull. Mr. Richards was exceedingly annoyed and lost no time in telling his H.S. she was in a disgraceful state of undress and furthermore it was an insult to her chief. If he could take the trouble to come to the hospital respectably dressed, surely it was not too much to expect that she should come to the theatre likewise. Mr. Richards ended his tirade by telling her to go back to her room immediately and not to return until properly attired.

On her way to her room, the rebuked H.S. met the anaesthetist, also in his pyjamas and dressing gown, about to go the theatre; but on being told of Mr. Richards' reaction to bedroom apparel, decided it would be expedient to appear in more formal gear. It so happened that the anaesthetist was of a 'prickly disposition', and, inwardly annoyed at having to dress properly, decided it would do Mr. Richards no harm if he had to wait awhile. If he wanted the residents to appear smartly turned out in the early hours of the morning, so be it. With this in mind, he shaved and washed before leisurely putting on his best suit and taking great care to see that his hair was well combed and with a nice straight parting. In the meantime, the female H.S. had returned to her chief in the theatre who was, by now, fuming at being kept waiting for the anaesthetist and demanded to know what all the prolonged delay was about, adding that it was gross bad manners to keep a chief waiting for so long a time. The poor H.S. had to explain that she herself had suggested that the anaesthetist should not come in his night apparel as it would not have been approved, and he had therefore gone back to get dressed in the usual way; so she supposed this was the reason for the hold up. After a considerable wait, with Mr. Richards becoming more exasperated as time passed, the anaesthetist eventually appeared, looking extremely smart in a smooth dark suit and not a hair out of place. He apologised for the delay, but explained it had taken him rather longer than usual to dress. Mr. Richards was bordering on the furious. But there was really nothing he could do about it. The night staff nurse was more than thankful when the operation was over and she saw Mr. Richards depart, in anything but a benign mood.

Although at this period, I regret to say, I could also be impatient whilst operating, with an occasional burst of temper, I think the night staff thought I was the lesser of two evils, and certainly on this particular instance. I suppose my outbursts of temper were due to a certain amount of tension whilst operating on difficult cases. Especially if faced with sudden profuse bleeding when the whole wound would literally flood with blood, I would wonder how I could arrest the haemorrhage. Fortunately these cases were rare, but when they came they were worrying in the extreme. I suppose, also, Mr. Brooke Hill's bad tempered behaviour in the theatre had rubbed off on me to some extent, even though it was now some time since I had been his H.S. At an impressionable age, a chief can influence his juniors for good or bad by the way he conducts himself, and the standards he sets. I was, in addition, still comparatively inexperienced and so anxious for everything to go well, aiming all the time for perfection, which I was gradually to learn is not always attainable. I would like to think that as my experience grew my outbursts lessened very considerably; I believe, in fact, that this was so. To their great credit the nurses never seemed to take offence or bear me any malice.

Part of my duties as R.S.O. required me to do a night round of the private patients - the hospital had a separate and modern block set aside for paying patients. At times my evening visits would be part professional and part occupational, as was the case with a charming middle aged man, a true aristocrat, who expected me to join him in a game of solitaire each night. He had undergone a major operation on his bladder, and for the first week or so all the urine drained through a rubber tube into a bottle at the bedside, the other end being in the bladder, none being passed at this stage via the normal route. After a somewhat stormy convalescence, he was more than delighted one day to find he had actually managed to pass a few drops normally, and from then on, each evening, I was met with a progress report, sometimes good, at other times disappointing. Soon a sufficient amount was being passed by the normal passage to fill almost a fair sized wine glass, although most of the urine continued to drain from the tube which remained in the bladder. Each evening, on my visit, I was shown the amount passed and my opinion sought as to the quantity in the glass - did I think perhaps it was a slight improvement on yesterday's? The operation had been severe and recovery disappointingly slow, and very naturally this was extremely worrying for the patient.

In those days, operations of this nature were relatively crude and a far cry from the present. I could well understand the anxiety of wondering if he would ever be able to pass water normally again, and putting myself in the place of the patient I am sure I would have felt the same.

I was met one evening with a degree of agitation I had not previously encountered. It transpired that he had had a sudden and intense desire to micturate. Unfortunately no urine bottle was ready to hand, and fearful lest the desire should go as suddenly as it had arisen, and there being no time to ring for a nurse, he decided there was nothing for it but to pass what little urine there was to come, into his table napkin which lay close by. Having done this, the wet napkin was deposited in the wash basin to await my arrival. I listened to this frustrating tale with sympathy, for as I have already mentioned, I could so well appreciate the anxiety engendered by such a slow convalescence, and the fervent hope that each day would see more and more coming from the normal passage as opposed to the beastly tube; unhappily this was not proving to be the case. I was, however, completely taken aback when he went on to say, "Dashed disappointing, having to pump ship into my napkin because now I can't tell what amount I've managed to pass, and it's so important for my morale to know. Perhaps you wouldn't mind wringing the napkin out into the usual glass and seeing how far it fills up!" Under the circumstances I felt I could hardly refuse and did as I was bid. The amount of urine which eventually found its way into the wine glass was disappointing, but as the patient remarked, a certain amount would have been absorbed by the material. I cannot tell after all these years, but I presume we then settled down to our nightly game of solitaire. I would like to have recorded that this most likeable patient went home passing all his urine via his penis, but unfortunately this was not so. He was discharged still draining from the tube, and I much doubt if he eventually did well. Operations on the bladder for growths at that time were often far from successful.

If this unfortunate patient left hospital only able to pass minimal amounts of urine normally, it was an entirely different matter with another patient upon whom I had operated for acute retention of urine due to an enlarged prostate gland. Not very long after he had been discharged I happened to get on a local bus and before I barely had time to sit down, I felt a welcoming hand on my shoulder, coming from a man in the seat behind. In a loud voice, and to a crowded bus he exclaimed that he was highly delighted with the manner his water was now parting, and went on to report that as soon as he had got home from the hospital he had gone into the back to piddle, and his missus, who was standing in the kitchen called out, "They aren't 'alf made a grand job o' thee. You haven't made the bucket rattle like that since our courting days!" Not content with this comment, he continued to discuss the various stages of the prostatectomy, and how he felt when it came to those young nurses doing things to him which he would 'never 'ave thought'! I was most embarrassed and seemed quite unable to stem his outpouring of clinical details. I suppose he was so delighted to be peeing with a real flush as opposed to a trickle, he just could not help telling the world. When it came to my stop I was greatly relieved to leave the bus.

Chapter Twenty One

Once again Christmas at yet one more hospital had arrived. There was really little difference, the one from the other. Same ward decorations, same anxiety to get as many patients as possible home, and the same round of parties, culminating in the Christmas dinner with Matron and the sisters and residents. That year we had a large number of bottles of drink given to the mess, including several bottles of sherry, which we considered to be of the cooking variety. Someone had the bright idea that they would be just the job for Matron's Christmas present, and, as all readily agreed to this excellent suggestion, they were duly dispatched, with the residents' compliments of the Season. When the day arrived for the Christmas dinner, Matron invited the residents to her sitting room for drinks before the start of the meal. When we got there we were a little taken aback to see that we were being offered the cooking sherry which we had passed on to Matron for Christmas. I think we all wondered if this had been engineered purposely.

At the dinner, as R.S.O. and senior resident, I was placed next to Matron, at the top of the table, though I would very much have preferred to have been, in a much less exalted position. I was doing my best to make polite conversation over the soup when, out of the blue, something splashed into Matron's plate and ricocheted off the soup into her face. This was followed almost immediately by a second splash, but this time I was at the receiving end. The table decorations included a number of small variously coloured cotton wool balls. One of the junior sisters had only too clearly not wasted her time at the sherry party (perhaps after all it wasn't cooking) and she was well oiled. Seeing the cotton balls, she thought it would be highly amusing to pelt Matron from her relatively lowly position, for, after all, what use had these balls other than ammunition? They appeared to be provided for the purpose. Both Matron and I tried to finish our soup as speedily as possible for the sister had got our range, and a cotton wool ball landing with some force in the plate can spread quite a lot of soup around. After a particularly telling shot, Matron turned to me, at the same time wiping a splodge of soup from her face, saying, "Sister does so enjoy herself at these dinners, and she is really letting herself go tonight." Fortunately, for the rest of the meal we suffered no further bombardments; possibly all the missiles had been used up, or the sister in question had been persuaded that it was not really the done thing to throw pellets at the Matron even though it was Christmas. I must say Matron took it all in good part and did not appear to be much put about.

At the conclusion of the dinner, unexpectedly, I was called upon to speak, and having no previous warning, was quite unprepared. So I fell back on the usual platitudes, and reminded the company that too many square meals make too many round people. Fortunately I had recently read a report of a nudist colony which came up with the original idea of holding a fancy dress dance to mark the end of the season - no easy matter for the unclothed! However, considerable ingenuity was displayed, and in the men's section the prize was awarded to a man who had extremely severe varicose veins of his legs - he went as a road map of Great Britain; and in the women's group, to the competitor who had placed a piece of string from one nipple to the other and went as United Dairies.

I thought this would be a suitable end to my unprepared speech, and hoped it would not be considered too risky, for the mixed gathering, though I was not sure Matron felt the anecdotes quite the thing. Despite my early and traumatic difficulties in making myself understood as a child, I now had no troubles at all in speaking in public, nor did I feel the least bit nervous.

The residents' quarters were by no means commodious, and all the bedrooms were in constant use. A few months before I arrived one of the house physicians had been taken ill, and as he was expected to be off duty for a while, a locum was engaged. This was unusual, for the normal practice required that the rest of the residents should double up and cover the work between themselves. Locums cost money and in those days there was always too little available. Having engaged a locum, the question arose - where was he to sleep? There was no room in the residents' quarters as the sick H.P. remained in his bedroom. The nurses' home was, of course, out of the question, so eventually the hospital secretary decided he should be put in a small side room off one of the older wards, providing only very basic accommodation. The residents felt this was pretty poor and thought the locum should be given a room in the very comfortably furnished private block, but the authorities would have none of this. They therefore thought up a plan to demonstrate their disapproval. Squaring the head porter, they were able to ascertain the likely time of arrival of the locum H.P. (head porters are always a mine of information), and shortly before he was due, arranged for a bed to be to be put up at the end of a little used hospital corridor; a ward locker served in lieu of a dressing table, privacy for this makeshift bedroom being provided by a couple of ward screens. It being essential to meet the new resident on arrival to show him his 'quarters', and as he was certain to enquire at the porter's lodge for direction, the porter on duty promised to inform the doctor's mess immediately. . In the fullness of time the message came and off went one of the house surgeons post haste. On meeting the young locum, who looked as if he had just qualified, the H.S. explained that he and his fellow residents felt they must lose no time in apologising for the sub-standard accommodation which the hospital secretary had allocated to him. It was quite true there was no vacant room in the residents' quarters, but still they felt strongly that some other and more suitable room should have been provided; they were very sorry about the whole affair, and furthermore, this kind of behaviour to locums could only give the hospital a bad reputation. The newly arrived locum looked utterly bemused, and when he was conducted to his 'bedroom' he could hardly believe his eyes. I am not sure what subsequently transpired, but I believe he went straight off to the secretary to tell him he couldn't possibly think of staying under such primitive conditions. The secretary, not aware of the residents' master plan, assumed he was alluding to the side ward which was to house the temporary doctor, and replied that he could see nothing wrong with the accommodation provided - surely he realised hospitals were not luxury hotels, and he was not 'staying at the Ritz'?

It is by no means difficult to imagine the misunderstandings which must have arisen between the secretary and the locum before the plot was unravelled! As I have mentioned, all this happened before I came on the scene, and during my time as R.S.O. there was no serious sickness and therefore no call for an extra bedroom; it would have been interesting to see if the hospital administration had learned their lesson, but I doubt it very much.

The resident doctors were a good lot and were always willing to help each other out if in difficulties, and at times they came up with some bright ideas. One in particular was most original. I was operating on a very sick woman who was bleeding freely from a ruptured ectopic pregnancy. Normally, the fertilised egg travels from the ovary through the Fallopian tube to the body of the uterus where it develops into a foetus. In ectopic pregnancies, however, the egg becomes arrested in the Fallopian tube and, as development proceeds, the slender tube becomes eroded, resulting in severe bleeding which proves fatal unless an emergency operation is performed. When I opened this particular patient's abdomen I found it to be full of fresh blood, the source of the bleeding coming from a ruptured fallopian tube, the extra uterine pregnancy being of some six weeks duration. The patient was extremely exsanguinated with a rapid, feeble pulse and low blood pressure; it was essential to get blood back into the circulation as rapidly as possible once the source of the bleeding had been dealt with. In those distant days there were no such things as blood banks; in desperate cases auto-transfusion was sometimes used as a life saving measure. I felt this was now the only hope for my patient and started trying to remove the large quantity of blood from the abdomen with a spoon shaped instrument which was proving quite inadequate for the task. It was then that my house surgeon had a brilliant idea - why not use the soup ladle from the residents' dining room? This excellent suggestion was immediately taken up and the ladle sent for, at the double, and after it had been sterilised proved to be admirable for the purpose. With its help I was able to ladle out most of the blood which amounted to more than a couple of pints, and having strained off the clots by passing the recovered and precious blood through fine gauze, it was put back into the shocked patient via one of the arm veins. This produced a dramatic change, and her condition improved from then onwards.

When blood banks and blood transfusions have been for so long taken for granted, it is difficult for the younger generation of doctors to visualise the very crude methods of the old days. Transfusions were relatively uncommon; there were no blood banks or transfusion services, and if a blood transfusion was considered really essential, the relatives would have to be sent for to ascertain if their blood would be compatible. The cross matching procedure was crude in the extreme - it involved placing a drop of the donor's blood and a drop of the recipient's blood on a white tile and observing the reaction. If clotting did not occur a pint of blood would be drawn off there and then and given to the patient, usually through a vein in the leg. If however, as was often the case, the blood proved to be the wrong group, further relatives would have to be summoned and the procedure repeated until a compatible donor was found.

At that time, the blood groups were labelled 1, 2, 3 and 4. The Rhesus factor was not to be discovered for many years, and compared with the present knowledge of haematology, the methods in use were amateurish in the extreme. It was not possible to obtain blood if an emergency arose while operating, and it was in these cases that auto-transfusion was occasionally used. The best method of retrieving the blood lost in the peritoneal cavity was by means of a sucker, but in the hospital at the time I write one was not available, and under these circumstances I quite fell for the idea of the soup ladle; it held an appreciable quantity of blood and furthermore, was easy to handle, and I congratulated my H.S. on his most helpful suggestion. This was not the end of the matter however. The Housekeeping Sister got to hear of the incident; presumably one of the maids must have mentioned it to her and she was most upset. She said she had never heard of such a thing we had no right to take away any of the dining room cutlery to use in the theatre, and how would we feel the next time the ladle was used for the soup, knowing it had only recently been used for ladling blood out of some woman's insides? I tried to explain that it had been sterilised, and had played an important part in saving a life, but she was not to be mollified. Shortly afterwards, a notice from the hospital secretary was posted in the residents' dining room stating 'in no circumstances whatsoever must dining-room utensils be removed for use in the theatres'.

Before leaving the subject of pregnancy, it was about this time that I came across a belief which I found it hard to imagine. I was explaining to a patient in her early twenties who had recently been operated upon for an ovarian cyst, that although one of her ovaries had been removed she would notice no difference whatsoever as the remaining one was perfectly healthy and would more than suffice for all her needs. I was taken aback by her reaction.

"I am so distressed at this dreadful news," she said tearfully, "now when I get pregnant I shall only be able to produce boys or girls, and I so much wanted one of each!" On asking what on earth she meant by this statement, the patient went on to explain that she had always understood that one ovary was for making girls and the other one for boys, and now with one ovary removed she would only be able to have but the one sex. I hastened to explain that this was a total myth it was certainly a new one as far as I was concerned, and it took quite a time before I could convince her it was sheer poppy-cock.

Once again my appointment was drawing to a close, and in a number of ways I would be sorry to leave, but the time had come to begin to look for a more senior appointment, as by now I had considerable experience behind me; the surgical ladder however, had yet to be climbed to the top. I had been quite happy in the hospital, and liked most of the Honorary staff. As is often the case, a couple of surgeons, apart from the 'great' Mr. Richards, had their eccentricities. The senior surgeon, for example, did not wear gloves when operating, claiming that his hands had greater sensitivity when not enshrouded in rubber.   Only if he came across pus in the peritoneal cavity, did he stop to put on a pair of gloves. He would remark, when this happened, "Sister, I am into pus, a pair of gloves, please." He also insisted on having a large sponge rubber mat to stand on, saying that it was much less tiring than standing on the unyielding terrazzo floor.   He was undoubtedly Sister's favourite surgeon and woe betide the nurse if the mat was not immediately forthcoming; needless to say, no-one else was allowed its use.

The other surgeon's eccentricity, if that is the correct word, was the over-riding desire to operate with ever increasing speed. When starting to operate he would look at the clock and remark, "Let's see if I can beat yesterday's record." This is the worst form of operating, and I am sure was done to impress the staff how fast he was, for it was usual, at that time, to equate a surgeon's ability with speed, which was considered a great asset.   Fortunately, with present day anaesthesia and the understanding of the importance of replacing fluid loss during major surgery, this no longer applies. What really matters is careful and gentle handling of the various structures, and a constant desire to complete the procedure as near as possible to perfection. Surgeons are individualists, some are naturally fast operators, others less so, and with experience they come to operate at the speed which suits them best.

The theatre staff, naturally enough, appreciated the fast surgeon as he got on with the job with no messing about and no time wasted. They were efficient and pleasant to work with. The sister had been there for a number of years, was not very attractive as regards looks, and was thought to be a bit on the sour side, put down by the residents to a disappointed uterus, which might well have been the case. Her staff nurse, however, was quite the opposite; vivacious and a good looker, and suffered from no such disappointment. Although I did not go out with her myself, she was in constant demand both from the residents and at least one Honorary, or so rumour had it. A house surgeon commented one day what shapely legs this staff nurse possessed, and when asked if that was the reason he liked taking her out, he replied, "No, but it goes a good way towards it."

I had become, as time passed, more aware of the physical attraction of the nurses, and had taken one or two out on the odd occasion, when doubtless some form of petting, on a comparatively mild scale, would have taken place, though I can remember precious little, and very definitely there was never any question of getting down to the real thing. I do not recall falling for any one particular nurse. The desire to increase my surgical capabilities continued to be my over-riding ambition, and I was, by now, becoming almost obsessed in my determination to make the grade as a surgeon, and already looked forward to the future when I would be in a position to organise my own surgical unit; even at this stage I had so many ideas I wished to put into practice.

I was very pleased, the week or so before I was due to leave the hospital at the conclusion of my R.S.O. appointment, to receive a letter from the nursing staff, thanking me in warm terms for the care and interest I had shown to them when reporting sick. They went on to say that I was the first R.S.O. who had offered such a marked interest and understanding, and they very mush appreciated all that I had done on their behalf. Not very long after I had taken up my appointment I was asked by the Home Sister to see a nurse who, she said, was not very well, probably a bad bout of dysmenorrhea she thought. In those days, this was almost invariably the diagnosis made with any nurse reporting sick with abdominal pain. When I examined the girl, I found she was suffering from a typical attack of acute appendicitis and, moreover, the appendix had perforated and she had now developed general peritonitis - a very serious complication before the days of antibiotics. I was furious with the Home Sister when I discovered the poor nurse had reported with acute abdominal pains two days previously at the outset of the attack, and she had done nothing about it. Only forty eight hours later, after the appendix had perforated, did she call in a medical opinion. I felt this was an appalling state of affairs and sent in a full report to the house committee, with the strongest recommendation that any nurse reporting sick to the Home Sister or her deputy, must be seen, without fail, that day by a doctor. I am glad to say this report was accepted in full and adopted forthwith. It was because of this unhappy episode that the nurses wrote their letter, thanking me for what I had done; but, really, all I had done was to ensure that, in the future, the nursing staff should receive the same medical attention as the patients whom they looked after with such devotion. But it was nice to know they appreciated my efforts on their behalf, and it is also nice to be able to say that the sick nurse made a good recovery.

I considered at this stage, and have continued to do so throughout the whole of my surgical career, that the nurses played a vital role in a hospital's good reputation, and their devotion to duty was worthy of the utmost support and encouragement in their great work. I believe the Home Sister's reason for neglecting to get a doctor to see a nurse reporting sick, was the desire to get her back on the ward as soon as possible, for nearly always there would be a shortage of nurses for one reason or another. If seen by a doctor, even though there might perhaps be nothing serious amiss, there was always the distinct possibility that he would advise having a few days off, and that would mean one less pair of hands on the ward.

Chapter Twenty Two

In order to continue the difficult climb up the surgical ladder it was, at this stage, necessary to look for a more senior resident appointment. Applicants were still required to be single even though, for this type of post, they would have been qualified for three or four years or more. I was fortunate as, without much difficulty, I obtained a position in a large and very busy hospital in the industrial north, which appeared to offer excellent opportunities to widen my operative experience. Up to this time I had no knowledge of this part of the country, and was somewhat taken aback when the lay chairman of the committee which had appointed shook my hand and remarked, "I hope you will be happy with us here."

To my reply, "Thank you, Sir, I am sure I will be." I received the unexpected rejoinder, "You can't say at this moment, wait till you have tried us for a bit." This, I thought, was the down to earth forthrightness of the northerners, and impressed me at the time. It was certainly common sense, for how indeed could I be sure when I had not even started ?

Although this was a senior post, I still had to be responsible for the resident doctors, which really meant keeping a check on their activities. I was soon to discover that my predecessor had been a strict martinet, and had taken on the posture of a headmaster, as opposed to the senior registrar of a hospital. On my first day, feeling utterly strange, not to say a little bewildered, I purposely did not enter the large dining room at the normal time of seven o'clock, but waited for ten to fifteen minutes before going in, thinking that it would make my first meeting with all the seventeen residents perhaps a little less formal with the meal already on the way. I was most surprised, and not a little embarrassed, to find the residents had not started their dinner, and were awaiting my presence with growing impatience. I had no idea that my predecessor had ruled that dinner must not start till he was present, except under exceptional circumstances. Moreover, it was my duty to do all the serving from the top of the table. Ladling out the soup was not too irksome a chore, but when it came to carving the joint for seventeen healthy appetites, it was a totally different matter, and by the time I had served everyone, when I sat down to start my meal, a number had already finished theirs. It was the accepted practice that no-one could leave the table without requesting my permission. I felt exactly like a duty master supervising a house dinner! I soon put a stop to this regimentation, and, at the same time arranged for the senior maid to do the carving, which enabled me to take my dinner in reasonable comfort. It appeared that, some months before I came, the residents' mess had got out of hand, and stern measures of discipline had been demanded by the Honorary medical staff when they appointed the previous senior resident - he appeared to have carried this out to the letter.

One incident of the past had particularly upset the hospital secretary. The jam at tea time, which was always the same and clearly of the cheapest obtainable, was placed in a large oval dish. A rather aggressive and impulsive house surgeon, seeing this dish with its familiar contents for the umpteenth time, proceeded to turn it upside down on the white table cloth, remarking as he did so, "I'm bloody tired of this same old muck; why can't we have some real jam for a change?" As was only to be expected, the doctors' maids were justifiably annoyed and reported the incident to the house keeping sister, who told the Matron, and she in turn asked the secretary to come and see for himself an example of the doctors' behaviour in their dining room, and to take a look at what one had done to the clean table cloth.

The secretary duly arrived and was extremely cross with what he saw, and sent for the erring H.S. forthwith. He told him he took a very serious view of this disgusting behaviour, and delivered an ultimatum that unless every trace of the sticky mess was cleared away he would be reported to the house committee, who would not fail to take an extremely serious view of this grave misconduct. He and his committee had every intention of stopping this kind of nonsensical behaviour. He gave the H.S. half an hour to clear away the jam; on his return he expected to see no sign of it, and woe betide him, if it hadn't been adequately removed.

The culprit, faced with the problem of removing a large quantity of jam from the centre of the table cloth, decided that the best and quickest line of action would be to treat the sticky mess as one would treat a localised tumour in the human body - by excision. He accordingly procured a surgical scalpel, and proceeded to cut away the 'diseased' area, leaving no trace behind, but in its place a fair sized hole in the table cloth. The excised portion he disposed of by throwing it out of the window! The H.S. later pointed out that he had simply been told to remove the mess completely which he claimed to have done. I am not clear as to the final outcome of this incident as I was not at the hospital when it happened, but I can well imagine the secretary's angry reaction when he returned to see if his instructions had been carried out to the letter, only to find a gaping hole in the cloth. By the time I was in charge of the residents' mess, the strict discipline of my predecessor had certainly had its rewards, for the behaviour was much more civilised.

As always in any hospital mess in which I have lived, there were the usual complaints about the food, which, on the whole, were uncalled for apart from the soup, which hardly ever varied, it had a sour taste and an unpleasant pungent aroma which someone remarked reminded him of unwashed socks. Under pressure from the mess one dinner time, I rang up the kitchen and spoke to the head cook. I requested her, on behalf of all the residents, please not to send up any more 'sweaty sock soup', and that was the end of that chef's soup of the day.

In those far distant days, all the house officers had to live in the hospital, and all had to be single, and, up to the time I arrived, all male. Shortly after I came, however, following a great deal of discussion, and not a little opposition, the first ever female resident was appointed as one of the house physicians. The majority of the old stagers viewed this revolutionary departure with great misgivings - it will not work, they prophesied. They did not appear to appreciate that female medical students were steadily increasing in numbers, and when they graduated it was essential that they should have an opportunity of obtaining an hospital post, otherwise they would be denied most valuable clinical experience.

We were fortunate in our 'first', for she soon proved herself to be really adaptable to living in an almost exclusively male mess, and quickly settled down quite happily amidst all the men, and became much in demand in brewing up numerous cups of tea at night, often supplemented by the luxury of scrambled eggs. The men were quick to see there was at least one advantage of having a woman on the premises, but she knew her rights and was not one to be put upon. Although she was a nice enough person, she was not very bed-worthy, and so far as I know there was no question of popping in and out of her fellow residents' rooms. In former times, if there was a suggestion that women should be allowed into a previously all male environment, invariably the question of the lavatory accommodation would be considered to present a real problem, and was not infrequently used as an excuse to defer the project. Not so however, in this instance, as it was thought the facilities were adequate and should be common to all. Not long after we had acquired our first female doctor on the house, I came across a notice she had pinned up on one of the lavatory walls, "Gentlemen should lift the seat, others must." As was only to be expected, before this notice was pulled down, another resident had added, "Stand closer, it's shorter than you think."

As I have mentioned, the standard of behaviour of the resident doctors had greatly improved, and, taken as a whole, was quite satisfactory; after all, they were young, worked extremely hard for long weary hours, and the occasional breaking out of bounds so to speak, was only a natural reaction to a life of considerable stress. Some letting off of steam was only to be expected. All the same, there were times when this youthful exuberance could be damned annoying. Fortunately, I was immune, being the senior and in charge.

One of the so called 'bits of fun' took the form of dismantling a fellow resident's bed. This would be completely taken to pieces, and the bed clothes, pillow cases etc., stowed in various places around the room. If the resident was comparatively fortunate, the disjointed bed parts would be left strewn about the room, they were the usual iron hospital type, no question of spring mattresses, and incidentally, linoleum covered the floor - a carpet was an unheard of luxury. If, however, the participants had been in a particularly 'playful mood', the bed would be taken out of the room and hidden elsewhere. This usually happened if the H.P. or H.S. was not popular. On looking forward to getting to bed after a hard day's work, possibly operating till late into the evening, it requires no imagination to appreciate the consternation, immediately followed by anger, of the resident on finding his bed had virtually disappeared, and the resultant sweat and frustration of gathering it all together again; worse still if the bed had been removed from his room. Retaliation was never easy, for nobody, of course, knew anything about it, and all condemned the practice as a cad's trick. No-one was ever caught in the act of sabotage.

One night, I was called out of bed by a very irate H.S. who, after a lengthy emergency operation assisting his chief, had at long last been free to go to his room, worn out and longing to rest his weary limbs. On opening his door he was non-plussed to find the room almost devoid of furniture - all that remained of the bed was the mattress, which had been placed on the top of an old fashioned and near decrepit wardrobe. It seemed to me that this was pushing things a bit too far and he had every reason to be annoyed. Although he was not all that popular, I felt I had to see he had fair deal at this late hour. I thought the simplest and fairest way was to wake up all the residents, with the exception of our female, and tell them to get up at the double and remake the dismantled bed, first locating the bits taken to the various rooms. This was not a popular move on my part, but it solved the problem and this particular incident did not occur again, although others arose from time to time.

On one occasion I was woken in the early hours of the morning by an almighty crash. On getting out of bed to investigate I found the large and very heavy sideboard from the residents' dining room lying on its side in the corridor. It transpired that there had been quite a party, and a few of the residents, having entered, too well, into the spirit of the evening, thought it would be a smashing idea to move the sideboard into the bedroom of an H.S. who they thought was still up operating in the theatre. He would be so surprised, they told each other, to find a large and heavy article of furniture blocking, the way to bed. It was far too cumbersome to be removed without skilled assistance and suitable conditions, neither of which could possibly be said to be present, and under these circumstances, not surprisingly, it had been dropped before the objective had been reached. It was some time before 'law and order' was restored. The senior night sister appeared on the scene as, hearing the row, she was afraid some fearful accident had occurred. Our quarters led into a long corridor which gave access to the wards, and although it was strictly forbidden for any member of the nursing staff so much as even to put foot into the doctor's corridor, ways and means could be found, especially when the residents threw a party.

On these occasions, favourite nurses, well up in the 'body unit' stakes, would be invited, and by hook or by crook would make their way to the mess, where dancing to a radiogram had been laid on, together with suitable light refreshments. At first, the room would be crowded with dancers, but as the evening wore on, fewer and fewer couples were seen to be on the floor, until eventually it would be all but deserted. I thought at the time, the exodus to the residents' rooms was reminiscent of rabbits seeking sanctuary in their various burrows following lively romps in the open. As the Resident In Charge I missed out on these amorous occasions, as indeed, was my usual wont. I felt I should set an example by refraining from asking a nurse to go to ground in my burrow. As a matter of fact, I do not recall having any particular desire to do so - yet one more example of my misspent youth.

There was a certain H.S. who arranged to enjoy a good night's work with an eager nurse, without the aid of the occasional mess parties - between them they considered they had worked out a most satisfactory modus operandi. On going off duty, the nurse would return as usual to the nurses' home which was a little away from the hospital, check in, and proceed to her room at the normal bedtime. Instead of preparing for bed however, she would leave by the window and make her way back to the hospital, and by careful timing, managed to slip into the H.S.'s bedroom where she spent the night, returning around six in the morning to the nurses' home, once more very skilfully judging her moves. There can be no doubt that the exercise was carried out with military precision, and the objective must have been considered well worth the risks involved. The entries and exits, contrived with such consummate skill, would in all probability, have remained undiscovered had she been wise enough to keep her mouth shut. As was only to be expected, with such an exhausting regime (not every night, only when the H.S. was not an call, but several times a week), she began to appear tired and bleary eyed, and inevitably her friends remarked that she was looking washed out these days. Was it on account of a long lasting and exceptionally bad attack of dysmen? This was too good an opportunity to let pass, for this particular H.S. was popularly considered to be the answer to a maiden's prayer.

"The Curse, my foot. I would think you would be looking just as, or probably more jaded, if you were in my shoes. Just try 'sleeping' with Casanova! Oh boy, how he gives you the works. What stamina, he's barely finished before he wants it up again!" Now, nearly always, talk of this explosive nature, in the fullness of time, circulates even though it is told in the utmost confidence between one nurse to another; possibly there creeps in an element of jealousy, and the exploits, so vividly described seen as a form of boasting. Whatever the reasons, it tends to be discussed amongst an ever increasing field, and it is only a matter of time before it reaches the ever watchful ears of the senior staff. Such was the case in this instance.

One morning, when the time came for the nurse to leave, having enjoyed as usual a night of multiple orgasms, and feeling well and truly satisfied, though somewhat exhausted, she was shocked, on stealing out of the resident's bedroom, to come face to face with the senior night sister, who, having got to hear of the time schedule, had been watching outside the door waiting to pounce. At this period, when discipline was extremely strict, a nurse found coming out of a doctor's bedroom meant instant dismissal: she would have to leave that very day. The H.S. would also be very severely dealt with, I have no doubt.

In describing certain aspects of the residents' behaviour, I have no wish to convey the impression that they acted in an irresponsible manner. After so many years have gone by, it is the odd and unusual happenings which tend to stick in the mind when recalling events which took place all that time ago. The daily devoted attention given to the patients by the house surgeons and physicians, who received only a pittance in pay, tends to go unrecorded. The hospital was first class, a splendid nursing staff, headed by a wonderfully good Matron, who saw to it that her patients had the very best attention possible. Taken as a whole, the resident doctors were also first class, and worked long hours without ever complaining, the well being of the patients under their care being their prime consideration. The Honorary staff too was excellent.

For my part, I was finding that my appointment gave me considerable satisfaction. I was kept busy helping the various surgeons, supervising the residents, and doing a fair amount of emergency work. I was also now being given major surgery to do on my own. Initially, I found this to be something of a strain. The day before I was to perform the operation, I would go over the various steps of the procedure in my mind's eye, trying to visualise any complications which might arise, and how to deal with them should they occur. Then, when the day came and I was actually scrubbing up in the theatre preparatory to starting the operation, I would have a last minute run through. Usually all went smoothly, and at the end I was left with a feeling of intense relief together with a gratifying sense of fulfilment. There were times however, when perhaps half way through a complicated and major procedure, I would be all but stuck; there seemed to be no way forward, and I had already passed the point of no return. (I used to liken this impasse to a climber who finds himself apparently stranded on a rock face, unable to proceed any higher as he cannot see further foot holds, and has gone too far to be able to retreat.) I could, under those circumstances, have sent for one of the Honorary surgeons to come to my assistance, but that would not have been considered a sign of competence on my part, except for a real emergency. I was soon to learn, when up against it, provided I kept calm, the most difficult situation usually resolved itself and the operation could be successfully completed. At times such as these, I was more than ever conscious of the tremendous responsibility which rests on the shoulders of a surgeon, and it made me more than ever determined to be as good as I possibly could at my job. I had already learned that there was no room for second best. Not only did I owe it to my patients, but almost equally to their close relatives. I had no wish, at any time, to betray the trust my patients placed in me when accepting my advice to undergo surgery, and I tried my utmost to observe this ideal.

Chapter Twenty Three

I had not previously come into contact with North Country patients and I very soon came to appreciate their true worth. Down to earth, certainly, but very genuine and outstandingly kind to their neighbours if ill, no trouble being considered too much when it was a question of need. The patients had, too, a very descriptive, if, indeed, not a dramatic way of expressing their symptoms. When I asked a dear old man how bad was his diarrhoea, he replied with considerable feeling, "It's that bad I daren't button up." I was to learn that the nurses' term for this unpleasant complaint was 'dia-rush'. Another patient told me his cough was, "That bad it fair knocks me out of bed." But the highlight for the unusual came when a somewhat dour and not very intelligent man, on his second visit to a surgical clinic, complained to the out-patient sister, that he had not been the same since that there doctor carried out a P.M. on him on his last attendance. A rectal examination was referred to as a P.R. - per rectum - both in case notes, and in conversation.

A further example of misuse of words arose in a hospital board meeting when a member, after a rather heated exchange, loudly announced, whilst banging the table, "Mister Chairman, from what we have just heard we are to blame, as a committee we have been far too laxative in the matter!"

As the senior resident surgeon I was at times called from the operating theatre to see urgent cases which had just been admitted to the wards. One afternoon, whilst operating, I received a message from one of the House Surgeons - would I go as soon as possible to see a patient with extremely severe renal colic, who was not responding to the usual measures and continued to complain of pain. Now true renal colic can be excruciatingly painful, and usually calls for an injection of morphia, if severe enough. This particular case, a man in his forties, said he was on his way south when he was seized with a severe bout of renal colic - he told the H.S. he knew what it was as he had previously passed a stone. The pain had been so intense he had been forced to come to the casualty department of the nearest hospital. The casualty officer agreed with the diagnosis and admitted him as an emergency, and in view of the intensity of the pain, ordered an injection of morphia. Despite this, however, he continued to complain of severe pain and this was the reason I was asked to see the patient. On examination he certainly exhibited all the signs and symptoms of intractable renal colic, rolling about the bed in agony as the spasms came at frequent intervals, his forehead and face covered with perspiration, such was the intensity of the pain. Moreover, he had just passed urine which obviously contained blood, truly a cast iron picture of classical renal colic of the severest degree. It looked, indeed, as if a further injection of morphia would seriously have to be considered. However, when I drew back the bed clothes I was more than a little surprised to note that although the forehead and face were apparently moist with sweat, the rest of the body was quite dry, including the arm pits. This was suggestive that the renal colic was phoney, and the patient almost certainly a drug addict - the commonest way for these wretched people to obtain morphia. They go to casualty departments throughout the country complaining of severe abdominal colic. Keeping a straight face, I remarked to the somewhat puzzled H.S. that this was an exceptionally unusual case. In all my vast experience (I laid it on to impress) I had never seen such an interesting phenomenon, profuse sweating of the face and neck, and the rest of the body perfectly dry - we must call the hospital photographer at once and get a permanent record of this unique case. In actual fact, the hospital did not run to the expense of a photographer, but he wasn't to know that! The upshot of this emergency admission of terrible renal colic was not unexpected - almost as soon as I had left the ward and returned to the theatre, the patient discharged himself; he clearly had no wish to have a snapshot which could be circulated to other hospitals, for these patients travel wide distances. It can, at times, be very difficult indeed to be sure that the pains are not genuine, and more often than not they get what they want. When I had finished operating I returned to the ward to make further enquiries and discovered that this particular addict with his assumed renal colic, had got his technique down to a fine art. On admission, he had called for a glass of water, and also stated he felt he wanted to pass urine - the while giving a very realistic picture of a true and very severe attack of renal colic. On being brought a bottle by a nurse he requested the curtains to be drawn around the bed, as he found it 'putting off' to pass urine in public. Having got his privacy, he proceeded to use the drinking water to sprinkle over his face and neck to resemble perspiration brought on by the extreme suffering. Having passed water, his next well thought out move was to mix a little blood, which he had brought with him, in with the urine (it may well have been butcher's blood). The presence of haematuria - blood in the urine - together with colic, is suggestive evidence that the origin of the pain is from the kidneys. Had the pseudo-renal colic not been correctly diagnosed, the chances were that this drug addict would have enjoyed quite a few injections of morphia. They become expert with the right symptoms and signs and are very cunning in the mode of presentation. The ward sister eventually discovered how this particular man had initially played his part so well, foxing the doctor who had attended him on admission, and had indeed obtained an injection before his sham had been exposed.

On an another occasion whilst operating I was asked to go to the out-patient department between cases to see a patient who had been referred to a medical clinic, but was thought by the physician to be suffering from appendicitis. At the time, our theatre kit consisted of green trousers and white vests. Not stopping to change, I put on a white coat and proceeded to the O.P. department, which was swarming with patients. There was then no appointment system, and the patients waited sitting on long wooden benches. As I entered the room where the Honorary physician was sitting, the sister overheard one of the patients, whilst looking at the clock, remark to another, "Just look at the time. It's past eleven o'clock and the house doctor is still walking about in his pyjamas. Is it any wonder we have to wait all morning to be seen? It's a positive disgrace!"

I have previously mentioned the excellence of the Matron. She was a good and kindly person, and was punctilious in doing a round of every ward at least once a day, and made it her business to speak to each patient, and to reassure herself that they were getting first class attention, which indeed, was universally the case. Usually all went smoothly, but on one occasion an embarrassing situation was narrowly averted. A patient, recently admitted, and prone to periods of confusion, would at these times pass his urine into the water jug by his bed, and not into the urinal provided for the purpose. To her horror, Sister saw this happening whilst doing her round with Matron, but really could do little about it, and none of the nurses had noticed. All she could do was to make a mental note to see that the jug was taken away at the earliest possible moment. When Matron eventually arrived at the bedside, as was her wont, she enquired how he was feeling. This brought forth only a rambling reply, but she gathered he wanted a drink. To the utter consternation of Sister, Matron proceeded to pour out a glass of what she assumed was orange juice cordial from the jug which had recently been demoted to a urinal, and to offer this liquid to the patient. Sister dare not tell Matron the jug contained urine for she would have got the 'Mother and Father' of a ticking off for allowing a jug of urine to be left standing on a patient's locker, and would hardly accept the excuse that it had only just happened. Fortunately, in his confused state the patient did not accept Matron's kindly meant administrations, and the supposed 'orange drink' went untasted. The nearby patients who were watching the proceedings had the greatest difficulty in keeping straight faces, but Matron continued on her way conscious of the fact that she had demonstrated to her nurses how important it always is to fulfil the patients' demands, even if it only entails pouring out a glass of drinking water.

Shortly after this incident I had the experience of a further misunderstanding. Sir Henry Stubbs, one time Honorary Physician to the hospital, then in his early 80's, but in his hey-day a well known and highly respected figure, came to the hospital and asked me, as Senior Resident, if I would be so good as to take him to the ward where his chauffeur's wife had been admitted with chest pain? Pneumonia. When we reached the ward I saw the double doors were shut with a screen across, the normal practice denoting that the ward was closed. However before I had time to point this out to Sir Henry, he was through the doors and asking the Sister in charge to take him to the patient. Sir Henry, though no longer a young man, still believed in getting on with the job in hand without let or hindrance, and he strode briskly up to the bed which was surrounded with screens. Sister barely had time to tell me the patient was on a bedpan before Sir Henry, ignoring the screens, was expressing his sympathy and wishing his chauffeur's wife a good recovery; he stayed only a few minutes and then withdrew. As we left the ward, Sir Henry turned to me and said, "I'm afraid that woman's ill - I detected a most unpleasant odour when I was at her side. I should think she is probably developing a lung abscess." I felt I ought to explain the real reason in case he alarmed his chauffeur unnecessarily, so I told Sir

Henry he had spoken to her whilst she was using a bedpan. Not at all taken aback, he dismissed this disclosure by remarking, "Was that so?"

As the months went by I continued to work hard and never a day passed without learning something new. I was happy in my job and was reaching the stage of feeling confident when operating, which I was finding ever more satisfying. When on call for emergencies, if I was not disturbed in the night to operate, I felt almost cheated of the further experience, I was so keen. Much later, when I became a Consultant Surgeon, and was called on many occasions for night time emergencies, I would look back in amazement at my disappointment at that time.

Chapter Twenty Four

As I have written on more than one occasion, I was an abnormally late developer as far as my relationship with the opposite sex was concerned. Up until now, practically all my thoughts and energies had been channelled into surgery, and I had had very little experience indeed with women, even though I had worked for so long amongst so many attractive young nurses and sisters. I was now to begin to put this right. It may well have been feeling so much more on top of my job that gave me not only more confidence with regard to my surgical abilities, but also more confidence in thinking that perhaps, after all, I was not such a negative person, though the memory of my wretched school days and unhappy childhood lingered.

I was becoming increasingly aware of an attractive staff nurse in one of the theatres, who, to my inexperienced eyes, not only had a captivating body, but who was also vivacious, and I began to take more and more notice of her. I had no idea at this stage what she in turn thought of me, but, holding the exalted position of Senior Resident Surgeon, hoped this might serve as a bonus point. In due course, I plucked up courage and asked Anne, having discovered her Christian name, if she would care to come out for a walk on the moors and then have dinner somewhere in the country. To my pleasant surprise the invitation was readily accepted, and we accordingly arranged a convenient day and place to meet, for it was not the thing to collect nurses from the home. First outings together are almost invariably times of mutual assessment, and the atmosphere is seldom relaxed. This proved to be the case, but after a tramp across the rugged country side, followed by a satisfactory dinner, helped on with a bottle of wine (I had still much to learn about alcoholic drinks), I felt more in command of the, for me, unusual situation, and Anne appeared also to be more at ease and less on her guard. On the way back I went so far as to stop the car in a suitable spot, and proceed to indulge in a little petting, wondering what response this would bring forth. To my pleasant surprise my overtures were readily reciprocated, and after a little while I found myself guiding Anne's hand to where previously only mine had worked. I appear to have given little thought to her feelings, leaving her, as it were, high and dry, but when we said good-bye Anne told me she had very much enjoyed herself.

It was inevitable that after this first outing, with its decisive conclusion, I should ask Anne to come out with me again, and equally inevitable, as she was no virgin, we should get down to the real thing, and as she put it, "Go the whole hog." At the time I was woefully ignorant of the importance of preliminary love play if the female partner is to achieve the fullest satisfaction from the act - all that concerned me was self gratification. I had no thoughts for the finer points. But Anne realised that I was a virgin and was most understanding, and with her sympathetic help I was soon to be able to make amends. I am sure she was more than a little surprised to discover how sexually inexperienced I was for my years. I managed to see Anne most days, and although undoubtedly sex played an important part in our relationship, it was by no means the sole attraction. I was coming more and more to enjoy being in her company, and as time went by we discovered we had much in common, and I found myself constantly thinking what a splendid companion I had discovered. There were times, indeed, when I thought of a life companion, but at this stage in my intended career as a surgeon I was in no position to think in terms of marriage for several years at least. I had no clear idea what Anne's were towards me, though I thought she must enjoy my company as she always readily agreed to come out with me, and entered into our various outings with obvious enjoyment. But I did not know if she had any deeper thoughts on our ever increasing friendship.

Anne was most attractive, and as was only to be expected, had had more than one ardent admirer from the medical staff in the past, and could very well do so again in the future. Moreover, she was an excellent nurse and a splendid sport. I was exceedingly glad I had got to know her so well, and I was finding she was now constantly in my thoughts. When we were off duty, we liked nothing better than to drive out into the country, which we both loved so much, and to tramp for miles over the hills and moors - a most welcome relaxation from the rigours of our work. We would often stay out for dinner, and on the homeward journey park in some appropriate spot. We seemed to be very much in tune with each other. For my part, I was becoming more and more drawn to Anne in a way I had never previously experienced. Although the physical side was a factor, this was by no means the sole source of my feelings - they went far deeper than that. Working in the operating theatres together served to draw us ever closer, and I was happy indeed, when, as a senior nurse, she helped me with a case. Garbed in my sterile gown with my hair encased in a cap, and my mouth and nose covered with a mask, I could look into her eyes without giving anything away, as my facial expressions were hidden behind the protecting mask. Although I felt fairly confident Anne liked me quite a lot, I was not so sure her feelings towards me were as ardent as mine were towards her.

I was now spending long hours in the theatre dealing with a wide variety of cases. Before the days of antibiotics, infections in various forms caused many problems. The one which was quite usual at the time, involved infection of the bones, the so called osteomyelitis. The primary source was often a boil or carbuncle, due to the common organism - the staphylococcus. Not content with causing an extremely painful lesion on the skin, in a small, but nevertheless significant percentage of cases, the staphylococcus gained entry to the blood stream, and was carried by circulation to one of the long bones, where it proceeded to settle and multiply, causing a very much more serious infection deep in the bone. When this occurred, the patients would suffer great pain, often associated with profound toxaemia. The only line of treatment available at the time was to make a long incision over the site, and to open up the bone in an attempt to drain the pus. Having done this, a large dressing was then applied over the gaping wound and the limb encased in plaster of Paris. The aim was to keep this on as long as possible. With pus soaked dressings under the plaster, it was not long before the patient was aware of an unpleasant odour, which steadily became more offensive as the days and even weeks passed, and it was by no means uncommon for the stench to meet you as you entered the ward. One day I received an urgent call to a patient who had been in for some weeks with osteomyelitis of his leg, and who was in an agitated state. The plaster had been on for a considerable time, and was smelling to high heaven. (It was thought the longer the plaster was undisturbed the better, despite the smell.) The cause of this patient's very understandable agitation was the alarming discovery of pulsating maggots in his bed. Feeling something tickling his thigh, he had pulled down the bed clothes to investigate, and was appalled to see a number of fat maggots crawling around; further investigation revealed that they were wriggling out from the top of the plaster which encased his leg as far as the middle of the thigh. No wonder the poor man was disquieted! I tried to explain that this did not mean that the leg had gone 'bad', (though one might have thought so from the stench), and all that was needed was a change of plaster.

In actual fact, it was found that the presence of live maggots was beneficial, for they ate up the pus and dead tissue, and the wound would be all the healthier for their presence. In my time, I have seen some really fine specimens, for they revelled in this type of diet! When it was noted how marked was the improvement, in cases where maggots had been found on removal of a plaster, at one time, maggots, especially bred for the purpose, were deliberately placed in the open wound before applying the plaster of Paris. They undoubtedly helped to cleanse the wound by ingesting dead tissue - maggots have a voracious appetite for pus! For a while this was a recognised line of treatment, and was considered superior to the more orthodox forms. The snag, as could so readily be understood, was the patients' reactions when the engorged maggots escaped from the top of the plaster to gain freedom amongst the bedclothes. It requires little imagination to appreciate the distaste engendered on discovering fat maggots wriggling out of the plaster, so, despite the beneficial effects of this line of therapy, which came to be known as the 'maggot method', it never gained wide support. The advent of antibiotics, as in so many other serious infections, has made osteomyelitis a rarity, and has completely revolutionised the management of this illness. My generation of doctors, who have seen the devastation caused by virulent organisms prior to the discovery of these modern drugs, can never cease to marvel at their effectiveness, and to look back on countless numbers of patients who would not have died had they been available at the time. It is difficult for the present generation of doctors, who take the powerful antibiotics for granted, to appreciate what we were up against in the old days.

Chapter Twenty Five

Many years ago there used to be a programme on the radio when the participants were asked, amongst other questions, "Now tell me the most embarrassing moment you have had in your life. You must have had one. We all have." If this question had been put to me, I would, without any hesitation, have related an experience I had when staying at a country hotel. Anne and I had now been going out constantly together for some time, and as we much enjoyed long hikes across the moors, I suggested we should spend a week-end at a small hotel, walking all day, returning in good time to enjoy a drink in the bar before sitting down to a well earned dinner and then early to bed. We were able to fix a week-end when we should both be off duty, and I phoned the hotel and booked two single rooms. Although I was officially off duty this particular week-end, my Chief at the time did not like being disturbed during the night, and apart from my annual holiday, expected me always to be available in case of real emergency, and it was for this reason I had left the telephone number of the hotel at the hospital before setting forth on what I felt sure would prove to be a most enjoyable week-end. I had been working long hours and felt I had earned a little relaxation.

All went according to plan for the first day and night; it was the second night things went wrong. Somewhere around two o'clock in the morning the hospital wanted to get in touch with me about an emergency and 'phoned the number I had left. The small country hotel had no night porter, and the manager, having no telephone bell in his bedroom, the telephone went unanswered. As the hospital wanted to speak to me urgently, they next rang the local police station, some couple of miles away from where we were staying, to ask if they could help. This entailed the sergeant being roused from his bed and cycling to the hotel, where he knocked on the front door. Getting no reply, he repeated his knocks with ever increasing force, but no response was forthcoming, the whole establishment seemed to be totally deserted. The sergeant was, by now, becoming increasingly frustrated, for he was getting nowhere with banging on the door. In view of this negative response, he thought a change of tactics was indicated, and decided he would try phoning himself, and proceeded to a nearby kiosk, but, like the hospital, got no answer. Returning to the hotel, by now understandably rattled but determined to wake somebody, with the aid of his torch he selected some suitably sized stones which he proceeded to throw on to an upstairs window, and by good fortune, happened to strike the manager's bedroom, who was awakened from a deep sleep by the sound of stones being hurled at the window. He got up, considerably annoyed, thinking it was some drunks intent on making a nuisance of themselves, and was quite taken aback to see a policeman standing below. When asked what was the reason for this disturbance, the PC replied he had an urgent message for the doctor from the hospital. Stopping only to pull on a thick pair of woollen stockings over his pyjama trousers, the manager went downstairs and opened the door to let in the Bobbie. The hotel register was duly consulted and my room number located, and with this information they proceeded upstairs. As knocking on the door brought no response, they entered the room only to find the bed unoccupied. Remembering that Anne had signed the register as well as myself, it was a simple matter to locate her room, and once again they both ascended the stairs and knocked on her door. Anne and I were together and were more than a little concerned to be disturbed at this hour and in these circumstances. As it was Anne's room, she got up, put on a dressing gown and opened the door to be confronted by a police sergeant and the hotel manager. Naturally taken aback, she misunderstood the question, 'Is the doctor here?' for 'Is there a doctor here?' and replied, "Yes, and a nurse!" The PC went on to explain that the hospital wished to speak to me urgently as one of the doctors had got out of his depth. I felt most embarrassed as, donning my dressing gown, I too got out of bed and presented myself at the door.

I can still plainly visualise the thick stockings the manager was wearing (I could not understand why he had bothered with these as the night was warm), and the sergeant standing there, complete with helmet and holding a large regulation lamp in close contact with his chest. It was a very sheepish doctor who was taken downstairs and shown where the telephone was, and a still more frustrated one when it was necessary to drive through the night to the hospital. In these enlightened times, an incident such as this one I have just described would be taken as a matter of course, but so many years ago this sort of behaviour was considered in a very different light, and definitely not the thing at all. Besides which, it was bad for the reputation of the hotel. All the same, it was done, but not openly as at the present time. I am sure the local policeman took a poor view of having his night's sleep disturbed, and would not think very charitable thoughts as he peddled the two miles home - mostly uphill. The annoying thing was that the 'emergency' which had been the cause of so much embarrassment could very well have waited till the morning. I was soon on my way back to the hotel.

I cannot hope to remember all the details of this escapade, but I suppose the hotel door must have been left unlocked for I seem to recall going back to my room, though it is doubtful if I slept much. I do however, clearly recollect having breakfast in the dining room; sitting at the next table to Anne and myself, was a man and his wife and their two children. The children had heard the commotion in the night and were full of it, keeping up a barrage of questions to their parents as to what it was all about, and what did really happen? Anne and I felt anything but comfortable; fortunately we were not drawn into the conversation. Although we had originally intended to stay three nights, under the circumstances, we considered it diplomatic to curtail our visit. I explained to the manager that it was necessary for me to return to the hospital - he seemed well enough pleased.

Anne, as was her wont, took it all in her stride though she clearly could not have enjoyed the experience. We had by now become very close friends, indeed I hoped, more than friends, as I was fast becoming extremely fond of Anne, to the point of falling in love with her. Had things been different in those far away days, I believe we might have become engaged, though I think perhaps Anne might not have been quite so sure of herself. But at the time, it seemed it could be some years before I could be in a position to marry, and I felt it was not fair to expect a girl to wait for an indefinite period, when, in the meantime, she could well meet someone who was in the fortunate position to marry and settle down immediately. During the period about which I am writing, if a man asked a girl to marry him, he was expected to have the means to keep his future wife in reasonable comfort. Unhappily for me, at this stage, I was far removed from such security. The training of a surgeon entailed the treading of a long and treacherous road, and even at a comparatively late stage along the trail, a consultant's appointment was by no means assured. We had lengthy discussions as to our respective futures, and the more

I saw of Anne, the more I wanted her for my very own, and she was constantly in my thoughts.

Then one day the blow fell. Anne told me that for the last few months, she had been considering applying for an exchange nursing appointment abroad, for a period of a year. She felt the experience would help her outlook as well as give her an opportunity to travel, and to see a little more of the world while she was still young enough to enjoy the fresh experience. It would also be a means of getting the wander lust bug which lay dormant at the back of her mind, out of her system before she finally settled down. After much thought she had submitted an application, and yesterday received word that she had been accepted, and was due to leave in four weeks time. Anne explained that she had purposely not mentioned this until it was a 'fait accompli', as she was sure I would have tried my level best to dissuade her from such an idea, and she felt, in her heart of hearts, that I might well have succeeded. She was, naturally, sad at the thought of leaving her familiar surroundings and her many friends, and especially sad at the thought of parting from me. It was, however, for only twelve months, and the time would soon pass - it would offer her an opportunity to take stock of our ever increasing friendship, and to test the old saying that absence makes the heart grow fonder. I was very distressed at what I had just heard, and even at this late stage, I entreated Anne to cancel the arrangements and to stay, but all to no avail. Having made up her mind to take the plunge, nothing I could do or say would alter her decision. As well as being distressed at this sudden and unexpected turn of events, I was saddened to realise I meant rather less to Anne than I had hoped and thought, for I reasoned that if her feelings towards me had been as mine were towards her, she would not have contemplated going abroad, even though it was only for a relatively short period. It could well be that absence makes the heart grow fonder, but possibly of someone else.

Anne tried to console me by saying we would be able to keep in close touch by writing regularly to each other, and when the year was up - and it would soon pass - we would be able to reconsider our future together, provided neither of us had married in the meantime. She personally felt we would find ourselves in the same bachelor states. She went on to say she had hundreds of things to thank me for, dozens of glorious outings into the country, dozens of calls at pubs, and many, many happy hours together, and she sincerely hoped I would not be too sad when...

"...I've gone, but my inner self will not let me do any other."

I was wretchedly unhappy following this conversation, and I hardly dared contemplate the future without Anne, for we had been, in recent times, so much together, and she had come to mean so very much to me. The few remaining weeks went by all too quickly, and as each day passed, it meant even fewer days remained before the dreaded day of separation dawned. I had decided not to go to the port of embarkation for two reasons. One was we both felt it would be too painful a parting, and the other was the difficulty in getting time off. My off duty times were strictly limited. On the few times I put in for leave of absence for a week-end, on return my Chief never failed to enquire how I had enjoyed my holiday. To have gone off in the middle of a working week would have been extremely difficult. When the dreaded day came and we had said our fond good-byes and she had finally gone, with Anne's last words, "Please always remember what happy times we've had together," ringing in my ears, I was utterly miserable, and felt that with Anne's departure my life had now been left with a painful vacuum, for her forcible presence had been with me so much of the time, and now it was no longer there. In its place was an empty void.

I attempted, in the days that followed, to fill this hurtful hole by working ever harder, for I was, now more than ever, determined to make a success of my career, to compensate in some small way for all that I had sacrificed. Despite all my efforts, I seemed unable to get Anne out of my thoughts for any length of time; so many things reminded me of the happy hours we had spent together, and I longed to have her back. I now knew, without any shadow of doubt, that I was very much in love. I kept thinking of the last occasion we had been out walking on the moors - it was a simply glorious autumn day, and we had eaten our sandwiches by a fast running stream. Afterwards we had lain on our backs soaking up the sun and listening to the soothing sound of the burn as it poured over the rocks. I felt very close to Anne and was saddened that this was to be the last time we would be together before she left. We talked of many things, there seemed so much to say to each other, even at this late stage. We decided, should we get married, we would like to have two children; a boy first and then a girl; and after discussing the possible names, eventually settled on Ian Alexander, and Elizabeth Anne. We promised to write regularly to each other, and hoped, by correspondence, despite the distance, to feel we were still close to one another. I told Anne, knowing her attractions, I was afraid she might well meet someone who would sweep her off her feet, and in no time at all she would get engaged. She reassured me, however, that this was most unlikely and called me a silly old thing for having such thoughts.

Chapter Twenty Six

It had to happen sooner or later, but when it did I found the experience profoundly distressing. Deaths on the operating table, which nowadays rarely occur are, indeed, traumatic events in the life of a surgeon, increasing still further the stresses and strains that are part and parcel of his work. Up to now I had been fortunate, for although I had operated on many so called bad risk cases, none had died in the theatre. When I did have a death it was quite unexpected, and so all the more painful, and affected me intensely. The patient was a man in the prime of life who was undergoing a perfectly straightforward operation which would not have kept him in more than a week. I had been operating for only a short while when the anaesthetist asked me to stop as the patient's pulse was getting weak and he was unhappy at the way things were going. I immediately ceased what I was doing and placed a pack over the wound. Meanwhile, the anaesthetist did his level best to resuscitate the obviously dying patient, but to no avail - all our combined efforts failed. An air of despondency settled over the theatre, as I hastily stitched up the gaping incision, and preparations were put in hand to remove the body to the mortuary. There appeared to be no cause to account for the sudden and unexpected death. Although it had in no way any bearing on the actual operation, I felt, all the same, that if the operation had not been advised, the patient would still have been alive, and this thought was to worry me, especially in the small hours of the morning, for I had given the advice.

As soon as it was clear that the patient was dying his wife was sent for, and I now had the hateful task of breaking the terrible news that her husband had passed away during the operation. Whilst I was walking away from the theatre to the ward I had ample time to visualise their last moments together. The night before the operation, at the end of visiting time, they would have kissed each other good-bye, his wife saying she would look forward to seeing him the next night, though he might perhaps be a little drowsy after the operation.

"There is nothing to worry about, you will soon be home again," she would say as she left the ward, giving her husband one last loving look as she went through the door. And now she would never see him alive again, and for her, his favourite fireside chair would be for ever empty. When I entered the small room off the main ward, I found her sitting on the edge of a chair, wearing an anxious expression, wondering why she had been so suddenly summoned to the hospital, when she had been told to ring at lunch time to see how her husband was after the operation. Whatever the approach, however carefully the words are chosen, it is virtually impossible to soften the awful truth when it comes to telling a close relative of the sudden unexpected death of a loved one.

In this instance, although I tried to break the appalling news gently as I could, initially, she didn't seem to grasp the fact that her husband had died. She repeated over and over again, "He can't be dead, he was always such a fit man and was in perfect health when I said good night to him." Then, when she came to realise, with dismay, that there had been no mistake and he really was dead, through her tears, she stammered out, "I wish he had never had the operation, if he hadn't he would be alive now." And then she broke down completely. Sister and I did what we could to comfort the poor woman, but really, what could we do in the face of such a tragedy? Sister produced a cup of tea, but under these circumstances nothing can alleviate the distress. I felt utterly impotent to help in the face of such total grief.

The rest of the patients in the ward were also upset, as, when he did not come back from the theatre, they realised a death had occurred under the anaesthetic, and they wondered if it could happen to them. All in all it was a most distressing time and I felt so deeply for the poor, bereaved wife. Once again, it brought home to me the great responsibilities falling on the shoulders of a surgeon. He it is who advises a patient to undergo an operation, and if a death should occur, even though it has nothing to do with the actual operation itself, it was on his advice the patient was placed in that position. Far worse, if the death should be attributed to an error in the surgeon's judgement. This was the first time I had had the unhappy experience of what is known as a D.O.T. - death on the table - whilst I was personally operating, and it had a profound effect on me. If the patient had been having an operation for a serious, or even killing, disease I would perhaps not have felt so deeply about the death, but it was neither of these. This occurred many years ago and, happily, such unforeseen tragedies are rarely encountered in these more enlightened days.

I was finding I was missing Anne even more than I had feared. In the past I had increasingly confided to her all my problems and anxieties, and invariably received sympathy and understanding, and more often than not, sound common sense advice. It was a source of great comfort to me, and faced with a difficult situation I had got into the habit of saying to myself, "I must ask Anne what she thinks about the position." And now, just when I wanted her more than ever, she was gone. In my heart of hearts I knew she would have told me that it had nothing to do with my surgery, and in no way could I be blamed; it was just one of those unexpected calamities that occur from time to time and, although exceedingly distressing, I must learn to accept them as part of the trials of a surgeon's life. But how much more consoling if I had been able to hear the reassuring words from her own mouth and to make contact with her passionate body.

Now that Anne no longer worked alongside with me in the hospital I was applying myself with even greater intensity to my surgical duties. Over the years I had carried out a very large number of operations, and at last experienced a welcome confidence in my abilities as a surgeon, and felt I had a sound foot hold on the surgical ladder. I was totally committed to my work and equally certain I would wish to do no other. My only worry at the time was the uncertainty of getting a permanent appointment as a Consultant Surgeon. Looking back over the years, it seemed a far cry from the days when I was a naive medical student, so very immature, so very unsure of myself, and ill adapted to the opposite sex.

Chapter Twenty Seven

In all the years I had spent in my hospital appointments I had been most fortunate in not going off sick, and, despite hard work, had enjoyed excellent health. But my luck was not to last. I started off with a bout of influenza - the usual symptoms of feeling rotten, high temperature, and profuse sweating. It was the winter months with a 'flu epidemic and this had depleted the surgical staff, so I did not wish to default in doing my stint of surgical emergencies. I hoped my night on call would allow me to enjoy an undisturbed sleep, but such was not to be the case, for around two o'clock in the morning a case of generalised peritonitis, due to a ruptured appendix, was admitted requiring immediate surgery.

When the telephone rang by my bedside and awakened me from a restless sleep, I lifted the receiver, hoping against hope, this did not mean having to get out of bed to operate, but my hopes were immediately dashed when my House Surgeon told me the diagnosis. Feeling far from well, I dragged myself out of bed and, keeping on my sweat soaked pyjamas, made my way to the theatre. Immediately I had finished operating, not waiting for the customary cup of tea, I hurried back to bed where I lay in a feverish state, being unable to sleep again. The next morning I was too ill to attempt to get up, and by the evening was seized with repeated rigors; at times these were so violent I felt I was being shaken apart. I remember next to nothing of the next forty eight hours, apart from being admitted to a side ward, where I was to remain for some weeks.

As a result of being called to operate whilst in the throes of an attack of influenza, I had contracted a rare and virulent form of double pneumonia, which had a very high mortality. Even after so many years I still vividly recall the agonising discomfort of that illness. With both lungs involved, breathing was fearfully difficult and very painful - at times I thought I was about to suffocate; the associated pleurisy meant that each time I attempted to take a breath I felt as if a sharp knife was being driven into my chest, and on the frequent occasions when I was overcome with a bout of severe coughing, the pain was even more acute. The nights, too, were an ordeal I came to dread. Despite large doses of sedatives I was unable to sleep for more than a short while, and I lay, unable to move from my back for what seemed to be hours on end. As the days went by with no apparent signs of improvement, rather a worsening of my condition, I began to think I might very well not recover, for I knew I was slowly but steadily getting weaker, despite all the treatment I was being given and the wonderful nursing care I was receiving.

Previously, I had never given the actual fact of dying any serious consideration. But, now faced with the possibility of death, I found myself wondering how I would react. I did not fear the process of dying so much; it was what, if anything, lay beyond, which caused me some apprehension. The unknown is always accompanied with a sense of fear. I once took part in a game; those who had not played it before were sent out of the room, to be led back, in turn, blindfolded. Those who already knew the ploy remained in gleeful anticipation. I remember, when it came to my turn to be brought back, unseeing, I experienced, as I entered, a pang of fear, as I had no idea what was about to happen to me. If I could feel like that in a mere party game, is there any wonder death should hold a strong element of fear; for there can be no turning back and no release of the blindfold - it is certainly no game to be played with levity. Such were my thoughts. I found myself, usually in the small hours of the morning, unable to sleep and feeling miserably weak, taking stock of what I had done with my life, and seeing mental pictures of those events which did me no credit. It was as if I were turning the pages of my life's album, the less creditable pictures staring out at me in stark contrast, and even though I turned the leaves over they remained.

For what appeared to be endless days of gross discomfort, interspersed with sleepless nights, at long last I began to show signs of slight improvement. Initially this would not last, and would be followed by a relapse, but as the time passed by, the improvement gained over the relapses, and I began to make real progress towards recovery. The days when I felt better, only to be followed by further setbacks, reminded me of the old game of snakes and ladders. Just when you appear to be ascending the ladder with steady throws, and the target is drawing ever nearer, the next throw of the dice sends you way back down the ladder, and you have to start the climb all over again. I coined the phrase - 'snakes and ladders' illness, and subsequently, when I had patients who were experiencing a number of setbacks, I used to tell them they had a snakes and ladders illness but I had not the slightest doubt they would come through for I knew they would not give up throwing the dice until the game was in the bag.

With such a protracted illness I was inevitably treated with a variety of powerful drugs, and, as a consequence, experienced at one stage very considerable gastrointestinal upsets. I was reminded of the definition of a brave man - one who dares to pass flatus when he has diarrhoea - when I did just that with disastrous consequences. I was, at the time, most uncomfortable, with gross abdominal distension, and felt that the passage of some wind - what the patients alluded to as a 'good blow off' - might perhaps ease matters. I should have known better, it was asking for trouble in the presence of intermittent diarrhoea. I felt thoroughly ashamed of myself as the nurses changed my sheets; as always they took it in their stride and couldn't have been more understanding. Although all were excellent, I discovered some were more gentle than others. This particularly applied to injections - with one nurse it might be a little painful, whereas with another it was barely felt. When these were being given frequently and for long periods, the added touch was very much appreciated. There is little doubt, when seriously ill, the criteria on which a nurse is judged rests on her gentle and caring hands; the less physically attractive nurse may well have the edge on the 'good lookers'. The pleasurable emotions of sexual arousal are effectively suppressed in the really ill patient; sex is the last thing that enters the mind, the struggle for survival is all that matters.

It is a different story, however when the patient is on the road to recovery - now his octopus hands are ever ready to attach themselves to the more glamorous nurses. The superb sister who looked after me so skilfully and with so much understanding, told me she knew I was going to get better when, one morning, I mentioned what a nice waist line she possessed. When I had first been admitted it had been considered quite on the cards that I would not recover, and I have no doubt this superb sister played a significant part in my survival. Needless to say, during this trying time my thoughts were very much with Anne, and I wished fervently she could have been by my side.

Chapter Twenty Eight

It was good to be back at work after so many months off sick. When I first started to operate again, my hands, encased in thin surgical rubber gloves of which, normally, I would be quite unaware, felt clumsy and the fitting rubber appeared to have been transposed to a thick woollen material. Not surprisingly, the delicate touch becomes appreciably diminished following a prolonged period away from the operating table. Fortunately, the surgeon's expertise quickly returns, as I was relieved to find, and I was more than pleased to resume the normal surgical routine which had been so abruptly terminated all those weeks ago. Having received the very best of medical and nursing care available, with everything possible being done for my welfare, I felt I must now try even harder to give my patients the same dedicated attention. Having had the best, it seemed to me to be only right that they should have the same, for clearly it would not do to expect something for myself which was not afforded to the rest of the patients.

Anne remained very much in my thoughts as we continued to write to each other. I was writing almost weekly, but her letters were spasmodic, and the intervals between seemed to be getting longer. She explained she was leading a very full life and had little time for letter writing. I was disappointed she was not a better correspondent for I so looked forward to receiving her letters, and read them many times over, always fervently wishing we could be together again. Then, what I had inwardly feared, happened.

After an even longer interval than usual, on returning to my room following an arduous day's work, I saw a letter in Anne's hand writing, waiting on my desk. Normally I would have been delighted for I so loved hearing from her, but on this occasion I had a feeling it bore ill news, and I opened it with apprehension. My worst fears were confirmed as I read, "This is rather an important letter and I have been trying to write it for a fortnight. Two weeks ago I became engaged. I hope this isn't too much of a shock. For some time I was quite unsure of myself, then the climax came rather as a surprise, even to me. Don't think too badly of me will you, though I fear you must. I hope I haven't given you the impression that I have embarked on this without forethought - we have thought and talked very seriously about it all. Forgive me for springing surprises on you like this - I hope you will do the same to me. I am convinced I am doing the right thing - I have never been so sure of anything, and I now know that to say there is no such word as love is wrong."

Apparently she had met her future husband, an executive in a good and secure position, at a New Year's dance, and had been swept off her feet, for she had known him for only a matter of weeks before accepting his offer of marriage. This was a body blow for me, for I thought so much and so often of Anne, and looked forward to the day when I would be in a position to ask her to be my wife, for I was quite sure we would be happy together. And now it could never be, she had gone from my life forever, and Ian Alexander and Elizabeth Anne must remain figments of my imagination.

I tried to put Anne out of my mind, but however hard I tried she would just not go away, and over and over again I thought of all the things I might have done to keep her for myself; perhaps, after all, I should have asked her to become engaged to me even though it would be an indefinite time before we would have been in a position to marry. It was so very different in those days from the present time when it is by no means uncommon for medical students to marry, and even start a family.

As the time passed, and my work load increased, Anne was less constantly in my thoughts, though she still remained with me on many an occasion, and I continued to miss her as much as ever; it is a stark fact of human nature that whatever is unattainable becomes ever more desirable.

I continued to work hard, giving of my best to the patients, and in return getting increasing satisfaction from my labours. I had now reached the stage when I could be considered to be a fully trained surgeon, and the time had come to look for a permanent surgical appointment as a Consultant.

Before the advent of the National Health Service, it was customary to call on a member of the senior staff of the hospital when applying for a vacant post. Sometimes you might be fortunate enough to have a chief who knew the senior surgeon, and he would accordingly write a letter in support of your candidature. On one occasion, I was favoured with such a letter of introduction, strongly recommending my appointment to the hospital staff. I was advised that it was important to go and see this surgeon prior to the date of interview. I therefore journeyed forth, and duly met this august person. He could not have greeted me more warmly, and told me he had been very pleased to hear from my chief, an old friend of his, saying how much he thought of me and my work. At the conclusion of a very pleasant meeting he mentioned that his son was also up for the appointment, but that would not, of course, affect the issue in anyway. When the day came for the selection committee to meet, and the senior surgeon's son got the appointment, his Father took the trouble to come and tell me afterwards that it had been a close run decision, and the committee had been most impressed with my recommendation, and he intended to write to my chief to this effect. I felt at the time the surgeon had been very tactful, and it was quite correct that his son should get the job, as he was, without any question, an excellent candidate.

This was but one of several interviews before I finally achieved my goal. I remember an occasion, when I travelled a considerable distance in order to meet the senior surgeon prior to an appointment, only to see him for a few minutes, and to be told I looked very young to be put on a hospital staff!

The appointment interviews were always a trying ordeal. Usually, six candidates would have been short listed from a large number of applications. When shown into the waiting room, my first reaction was to appraise the chance of success against the competition of the other candidates: usually at least one or two would appear to pose formidable opposition. We behaved in a somewhat strained manner, for each appeared as a threat to the other's hopes of appointment. After we had all been interviewed, and this could take some considerable time, there was an anxious wait whilst the committee made up its mind as to the most suitable applicant. Once again this could take up to half an hour or more. We hopeful future surgeons would wait anxiously with mounting apprehension as the minutes dragged on. At long last, the doors would open, and the secretary would ask the successful applicant to return to the committee room, to be offered, by the Chairman, the appointment which we all so much coveted. The rest were left disappointed and dispirited. In the course of time the secretary would reappear to say his committee had had a very hard decision to make, as all the applicants had been of such a high calibre, and to thank them for their attendance. He felt sure they would soon be successful elsewhere - this was the usual gentlemanly way of attempting to put a little sugar on the bitter pill of disappointment.

Consultant appointments are not lightly made. Once appointed to a hospital the surgeon is there for life. It is no easy matter to assess the various qualities of a candidate in a comparatively short space of time, for not only must a surgeon possess the necessary expertise, to be able to perform a diversity of operative procedures, he must also know when and when not to operate - most important decisions and calling for considerable experience. In addition, personalities have to be appraised, for a difficult character may very well disrupt the harmony of the hospital. It is no wonder then, that the applicants have to wait in agony whilst these important decisions are made, for they are, only naturally, anxious to get their reward, having spent so many years working long and arduous hours to gain the expertise and experience which plays so vital a role in a surgeon's life. This may not, at times, be fully appreciated as was certainly the case of a self-made business man who returned his surgeon's account with an enclosed letter requesting that the fee for having his appendix out be considerably reduced. He wrote, "I understand the operation took little over half an hour and you have charged £50. I have no intention of paying you that amount of money for just 30 minutes work. I await your amended bill." In due course the account was returned and amended to read, "To removing the appendix £5.

To knowing how to remove it £45."

After so many years of toil and sweat, it was indeed gratifying to have achieved my ultimate aim, more especially having regard to my earlier slow development, when the future looked so very bleak. I have been for ever grateful to my medical training; if I made it, it had certainly made me. Now, at long last, I was in a position to put into practice all the things I had thought about during the long years of my training. I realised, however, it would not always be an easy road to tread, and it would be a mistake to attempt too much too quickly. My aim, now I was my own boss, was to convey to the patients under my care the simple fact that they were guests for the duration of their illness, and not just impersonal occupants of a bed. I had tried to do so previously, but now I was in complete charge, it would be so much more satisfactory in every way.

For some years I had made it my routine to go and see the patients in the anaesthetic room before they were anaesthetised, in order to check in on the notes, and to reassure the patient - they were not usually so heavily pre-medicated not to appreciate what was going on. I would say, "Now there is nothing to worry about, we will have you safely back in bed before you know anything about it; and everything is going splendidly, today," or words to that effect. I felt strongly that this was an important part of a surgeon's duties and many patients told me afterwards, when recovering from their operations, how they had appreciated this human touch and how reassured they had been at the time. I was to continue this practice throughout the years, and I instructed my registrars to do the same.

Having been appointed a Consultant Surgeon, I had every intention of trying to make a success of my surgical career, and to get as far as it was possible up the ladder towards the top. The senior surgeon in my last hospital, a very much 'down to earth' man, was fond of telling his house surgeons and registrars, how his Mother had repeatedly urged him to work hard so as to be sure of getting to the top of his profession. But what she didn't tell him, having got to the top of the tree, you had to hang on like 'bloody hell', as there were 'a lot of little buggers below trying to shake you off'. He was most definitely a character and made sure no-one dislodged him from his lofty perch. As well as being a character, he possessed a down to earth approach to his patients, and did not beat about the bush. If he suspected that a patient's multiple and varied symptoms were possibly neurotic in origin, he would ask, "Do you experience a peculiar tingling sensation at the back of your neck when you are passing water?" If the patient replied, "Yes, doctor, I do," he or she was referred forthwith to a psychiatrist.

There was another surgeon on the staff who had a 'thing' about his patients being over weight. On seeing a fat patient, he would insist that they lost weight before he would operate, and to this end, handed out a strict diet sheet, at the same time telling them they were digging their own graves with their knives and forks. The surgeon himself was a fitness addict, of slim build, and expected his patients to follow his example. On one memorable occasion he had operated in a nursing home on an over weight patient for a rupture, and after the operation had stressed the importance of going on a strict diet, and now was a heaven sent opportunity. After a few days, the poor patient found he was missing his normal meals very much, and one morning, feeling extra hungry, after a great deal of persuasion, he managed to get the Sister in charge, as a very special treat, to bring him bacon and eggs for breakfast in place of the ordered glass of orange juice and a thin slice of toast. He was just starting to enjoy this rare treat to the full, when, to his horror, he heard his surgeon talking to a nurse outside his room. Thinking that, as it was early, it would only be a quick courtesy visit and not really a profession call, with great presence of mind, he just had time to slip the plate of half consumed bacon and egg inside the bed clothes before the surgeon entered. To the consternation of the patient, instead of the expected, "Good morning, everything all right? I will be in later to look at the dressing," he advanced to the bed and, without more ado, pulled down the sheet and blanket to view the operation site and was more than taken aback when the plate of forbidden fare was revealed reposing on the patient's abdomen. Deadly silence reigned. The tension was broken by the Sister remarking, "That's the first time in my nursing experience I've seen a fried egg on the wrong side of the blanket!" The surgeon, though by no means pleased, added, "You had better finish your breakfast before it gets cold, the bedclothes won't keep it as warm as the orthodox hot plate." He must have realised that it is not every day a surgeon discovers bacon and egg in a patient's bed, and the episode would, no doubt, come in useful as an after dinner story. The sister in question had a good sense of fun. Once, when a patient was being discharged following removal of his prostate causing acute retention of urine, she presented him with bunch of sweet peas with her blessings for the future.

I have mentioned the characteristics of two of the surgeons in my last hospital, the one explaining the difficulties of remaining at the top of the tree, and the other the dangers of adiposity. There was also a third member of the staff, nicknamed by the residents 'the Accountant' as he was so keen on the nurses' figures, who was fond of expounding to his juniors the adage of the three essentials for eventual success as a consultant. They were, he said, "Firstly, a bald head to give an air of wisdom. Secondly, a protuberant abdomen to give an air of prosperity. And thirdly, a painful pile to give an air of anxiety. Clearly, at the outset of my consultant career, I could hardly hope to qualify on any of these three counts, but despite the physical drawbacks, I was determined to do my utmost to justify my appointment to the hospital staff. My work was now my whole life, and afforded me much happiness, though I still missed Anne. I came to feel more and more, as time passed by, the loss of someone to share the pleasures and sorrows which inevitably accompany the work of a surgeon, and deeply regretted I was not so blessed.

In an attempt to compensate for this lack, I spent more and more of my time in the hospital wards and operating theatres, which afforded me great satisfaction. And now all this is in the past. As the years roll on with ever increasing speed, and the three score years and ten continue to be exceeded, I look upon my next birthday as being the first day of the rest of my life. I only wish I had known so much more of the facts of life when I was young, and had not wasted all those years of opportunities. I feel I could have made more of my life than I have done. I suppose, though, it is by no means unusual to think these thoughts - to think otherwise must surely smack of self satisfaction. As my surgical days fast recede into the distant past, I am reminded that -

When the hair turns grey and the teeth decay,
And the mind makes appointments the body can't keep
Then it's time to prepare for your last long sleep.